easy kids knits

easy kids knits

clothes and accessories for 3–10-year-olds

Claire Montgomerie

with photography by Sandra Lane

RYLAND
PETERS
& SMALL

LONDON NEW YORK

Senior designer Sonya Nathoo
Senior editor Sarah Hoggett
Location research Emily Westlake
Production Ros Holmes
Art director Leslie Harrington
Publishing director Alison Starling

Indexer Hilary Bird
Pattern checker Marilyn Wilson
US consultant Eleanor Van Zandt

First published in the
United Kingdom in 2009 by
Ryland Peters & Small
20–21 Jockey's Fields
London WC1R 4BW
and in the USA
by Ryland Peters & Small, Inc.
519 Broadway, 5th floor,
New York, NY 10012
www.rylandpeters.com

10 9 8 7 6 5 4 3 2 1

Text © Claire Montgomerie 2009

Design and photographs
© Ryland Peters & Small 2009

ISBN: 978-1-84597-882-2

A CIP record for this book is available from
the British Library.

Library of Congress Cataloging-in-Publication Data

Montgomerie, Claire.
  Easy kids knits : clothes and accessories for 3-10-
year-olds / Claire
Montgomerie ; with photography by Sandra Lane.
     p. cm. -- (Easy kids knits)
  Includes index.
  ISBN 978-1-84597-882-2
  1. Knitting--Patterns. 2. Children's clothing. I. Title.
  TT825.M6624 2009
  746.43'20432--dc22
                                    2009010302

Printed and bound in China

PICTURE CREDITS
All photographs by Sandra Lane except the following
by Claire Richardson:
Pages 2, 5, 10–12, 13 (top left and right, bottom left),
14–15, 17, 20–22, 24, 26, 27 (top and center), 28–29,
30, 35, 36–37, 38–39, 124.

contents

introduction

After the publication of my first book, *Easy Baby Knits*, I found that some new mothers who had used it to learn to knit wanted to make clothes for their growing children—but there seemed to be fewer patterns available for kids over two years old. This gave me the idea for a follow-up collection of designs for three- to ten-year-olds. As with *Easy Baby Knits*, my aim has been to keep the patterns simple and wearable, yet modern and interesting. I have tried to design garments and accessories for almost every occasion, from sweaters and scarves for playing out in the park on a chilly day to pretty cover-ups to wear with summer party dresses.

Easy Kids Knits is aimed at beginner and more experienced knitters. In addition to patterns using the basic stitches, I've also included simple cabling and lace knitting, as well as knitting in the round. I have tried to choose yarns that are durable yet comfortable to wear. Most of the designs in *Easy Kids Knits* use yarns with a luxurious blend of natural and man-made fibers; the natural fibers create a soft and breathable fabric, while the man-made ones provide durability and in many cases allow the resulting garments to be machine washed.

It was great fun compiling the colorful palette for the designs, as I felt children deserve a bold and bright wardrobe to stimulate them and suit their playful nature. There are rainbow stripes, hot pinks, and deep greens and blues, as well as neutrals, taking advantage of the wealth of beautiful yarn colors available today.

My aim in *Easy Kids Knits* has been to provide a sophisticated yet fun compilation of original patterns that are interesting to make, comfortable to wear, and stylish. I hope that you will enjoy making them. Most importantly, I hope that the children for whom you make them will take pleasure in wearing them.

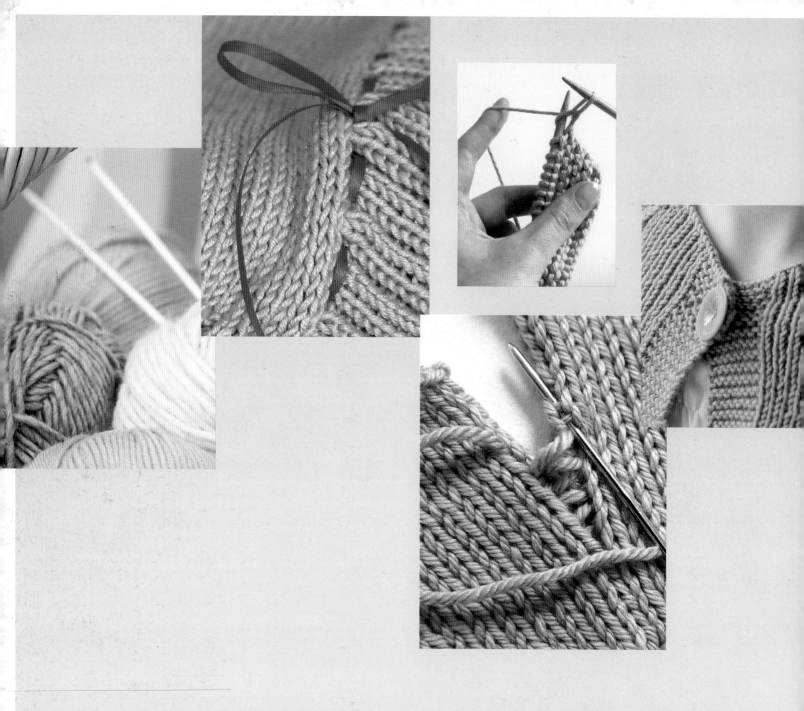

getting started

essential equipment

Knitting needles and yarn are obviously the most important things you need when knitting, but there are also other knitting tools. Some, such as cable needles, relate to specific knitting techniques, while others are more general. Here are some of the most useful; all are inexpensive and readily available.

knitting needles

Needles are made from many materials—bamboo, metal, plastic, casein, and different types of wood. If you're a complete beginner, I recommend that you start with bamboo needles, as they are more pliable than needles made from other materials and so are kinder on your hands. There is also less chance of accidentally dropping stitches, as the stitches cling to the bamboo more readily than to other needles. The material that the needles are made from does not affect the appearance of the stitches, so it really doesn't matter what kind you use. However, it can affect the gauge (tension), so don't change to a different type halfway through a project.

Knitting needles also come in different lengths, in order to accommodate different numbers of stitches. Again, the length of needle that you use is purely down to personal preference, and you will discover this with experience. The size of needle you choose is determined by the weight (or thickness) of the yarn you are using. The needle size refers to the diameter of the needle; generally, thicker yarns need bigger needles. A recommended needle size will usually be shown on the yarn ball of your chosen yarn.

Straight needles for normal knitting usually have a pointed end and a stopper at the other, to prevent stitches from falling off,

marker pins

buttons

row counter

but other needles are pointed at both ends. These double-pointed needles, or dpns, ensure that the stitches can be worked from either end and are used for knitting seamless fabrics in the round. Dpns are not used in pairs but in multiples of four or five, with three or four working needles holding the stitches and one needle being used for knitting (see page 32).

Circular needles can also be used for knitting in the round. These needles are two regular, shortened needles joined together by a nylon cable of differing lengths. Circular needles can also be used for knitting straight and are especially useful for projects such as blankets, when you have large numbers of stitches to work across. The bulk of the stitches can sit on the cable, so the cable takes the weight of the fabric, making it more comfortable to knit.

If you are planning to do aran, or cable, knitting (see page 33), you will need a cable needle to store some stitches safely while you are knitting others. Cable needles are like a very short dpn, pointed at both ends. Some are straight; others have a v- or u-shaped kink to ensure that the stored stitches remain on the cable needle while you are not using them.

other equipment

Other essential items include a pair of sharp embroidery scissors for cutting yarn, a tape measure, and a large tapestry needle, or yarn needle, which has a blunt point for sewing seams and weaving in yarn ends. Stitch holders are useful for keeping un-worked stitches safe until they are needed. The best kind are double-ended, so that you can knit the stitches straight off the holder instead of placing them back on the needle, but you can use safety pins to hold just a few stitches.

A row counter is not essential, but is handy if you find you keep losing track of how many rows you have knitted. Stoppers prevent the stitches from falling off the needle in your workbox if you are in the middle of a project. Stitch markers are used to mark a position in your work that you will have to refer back to, such as where you have to begin to sew in a sleeve. Large-headed marker pins are useful for holding seams together and for blocking (see page 36). If your design requires buttons, it is worth spending time choosing ones that work well on the garment you have put time and effort into making. Finally, a crochet hook is a great tool to have at hand in dropped-stitch emergencies!

stopper

stitch holder

stitch marker

yarns

There is a wonderful range of knitting yarns on the market, both natural and man-made. As a general rule, natural yarns, which are made from animal and plant fibers, are more pleasant to wear and easier to knit with, whereas man-made yarns are often cheaper, more durable, and easier to care for.

Yarns come in varying weights and textures. The most common weights are lace (1-ply), fingering (2-ply or 3-ply), sport (4-ply), light worsted (double knitting, or DK), fisherman/worsted (aran), chunky, and bulky. The thickness of a yarn is defined by the number of strands (or plies) spun together to make it. As the thickness of the plies can vary, two yarns that arre nominally the same weight, but different brands, may vary in thickness.

The plies can be spun tightly or loosely to create different qualities, such as softness from a loose twist or strength from a tight twist. If you are a beginner, be careful with loose twists, as the points of the needles can sometimes go through the yarn instead of through the stitch. The spinning process can also create textured yarns such as slub, gimp, bouclé, and other fancy types, which can create wonderful textures when knitted but can also be far more difficult for a novice to work with, so again be careful with these. Novelty yarns, such as ribbon, eyelash, furry, and metallic yarns, should also be treated with caution at first, as the stitches can be hard to define, and so it is easier to make a mistake.

pulling yarn from the inside

When you begin a project, take the working end of the yarn from the inside of the ball, as shown. This stabilizes the ball of yarn. If you start knitting with the outside end of the ball, the ball may roll around too much and eventually knot. It can be fussy digging out the inside end, but it is worth doing—although the outside end will do the same job. If your yarn is in a skein, wind it into a ball before use to prevent knotting.

pulling yarn from the inside

holding needles and yarn

Method 1: Holding the needle like a pen

Method 2: Holding the needle like a knife

Holding yarn, English way
Wrap the ball end of the yarn around your little finger. The yarn then passes under the two middle fingers and over the forefinger.

Holding yarn, Continental way
Wrap the yarn around the middle or little finger of your left hand, then pass it over the forefinger of the same hand, keeping the yarn taut.

holding needles

There are no hard-and-fast rules about how to hold the needles, but if you follow the suggestions on these pages, you will find that you can keep a steady pace and work with even tension. The most common methods are to hold the needles like a pen (Method 1), or like a knife (Method 2). You may find that both hands want to hold the needles in the same way, or that your right hand wants to hold the needle like a pen and the left hand like a knife, or vice versa. Use whichever method feels most comfortable.

holding yarn

It is important to maintain an even tension; this is governed by the way you hold the yarn and control its flow. Depending on whether you use the English or the Continental method of knitting (see pages 22–23), you will hold the yarn in either your right or your left hand, respectively. In either case, you need to wrap it around your fingers (see photos, left). If you are left-handed, you may find the Continental method easier, as the work is more evenly divided between the two hands; some left-handed knitters use the English method reversed, holding the yarn as shown, but in the left hand.

making a slip knot

Now that you are holding the needles and yarn properly, you are ready to begin knitting. The first thing you need to learn is how to make a proper slip knot; this is the foundation of your knitting, whichever method of casting on (placing the stitches on the needle) you employ.

A slip knot is basically what it sounds like—a neat knot that can slip to the correct size to fit around any needle. The slip knot will also be your first stitch.

You need to make the slip knot some distance from the loose end of the ball of yarn; the amount of yarn that you leave before you make the knot depends on the type of cast-on that you are using (see pages 16–19). If in doubt, leave more yarn than you think you will need; you will find that this is something that you will get better at judging with practice.

Making a slip knot is simple; all the same, it's a good idea to practice it several times before you move on to casting on so that the technique is firmly embedded in your mind.

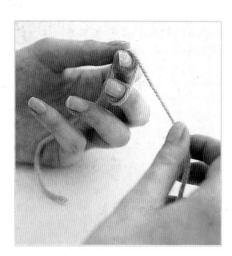

1 Wrap the ball end of the yarn around your first two fingers to create a ring and hold it in place with your thumb.

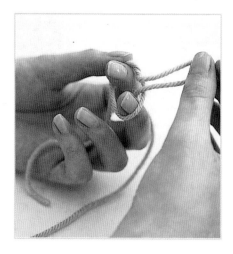

2 Working from the ball end of the yarn, form a loop of yarn in your fingers and carefully pull it through the ring.

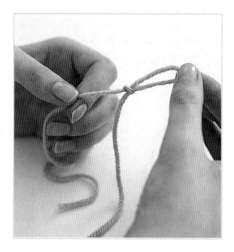

3 Holding the loop and the loose end of yarn tightly, pull firmly to tighten the slip knot. You can now put a needle through this loop and pull one end of the yarn to tighten the loop to fit the diameter of the needle.

casting on

Before you can begin any knitting project, you need to get the required number of loops, or stitches, onto the needle—a process known as casting on. There are many different ways of casting on; here are three of the neatest and most useful.

As you develop as a knitter, you can search out other techniques, especially if a pattern requires a specific cast-on method. When a pattern does not specify how you must cast on, you can use your favorite method—so it is worth trying them all to see which you find easiest and which gives your favorite edge.

Before you cast on for your first project, spend some time practicing by casting on as many stitches as you can and then pulling them off the needle and starting again until you feel confident that you have mastered the technique. It is easy to forget how to do it, as you only cast on once, right at the beginning of a piece, and it may be some time before you need to cast on again for another project.

The most important thing to remember when casting on is that you need to create an edge that is not too tight, as this will affect the neatness of the edge and put a lot of extra tension onto the cast-on. With this in mind, whichever method you adopt, try to keep the loops as loose as possible, without being baggy. If you find this difficult, try casting on with needles that are just slightly larger than those required for the rest of the fabric, remembering to change to the correct needles directly afterward, before you knit the first row.

casting on: thumb method

This method creates an even, stretchy edge. It is less noticeable than other methods, as it looks like a row of knitted stitches, although it is not counted as the first row.

Here, only one needle is used. The needle is held in the right hand, with the thumb of the left hand acting as the left needle. This method of casting on is for English-style knitters only, as you must hold one strand of yarn in your right hand and effectively knit with it (see page 22). The same effect can be produced by the Continental method, which is shown on page 18. With either method, you need to remember to leave a tail of yarn after the slip knot that is long enough to complete the cast-on row. This tail should be roughly five times as long as the number of stitches that you will be creating.

thumb method

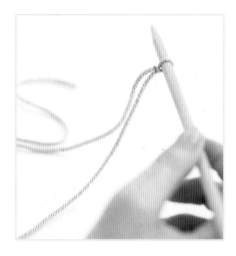

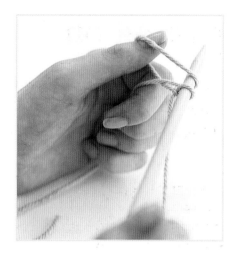

1 Make a slip knot, leaving a tail of yarn before it about five times the width of the cast-on edge. This is something you will get better at judging with practice. Slip the knot onto a needle in your right hand and tighten it to the right size.

2 Grab the loose end of the yarn in your left hand and make a loop around your left thumb, as shown, still holding on tight to the loose end. Wrap the ball end of the yarn around the fingers of your right hand, as shown on page 13.

3 With your left thumb upright, pass the needle under the loop, from bottom to top.

4 With your right hand, wrap the ball end of the yarn around the needle, and pass the yarn underneath and then over the point. Hook the loop on your thumb over the point of the needle, as shown here.

5 Pull gently on the loose end of the yarn to draw the loop tightly around the needle. Your first cast-on stitch is complete, and, together with the slip knot that you made in Step 1, you now have two stitches on the needle.

6 Repeat from Step 2, winding the yarn around your thumb to make the next stitch, until you have the correct number of stitches on the needle. When you begin to knit the first row, remember to use the ball end of the yarn to knit with, not the loose end left over from casting on.

casting on: continental method

The Continental method is a different means of creating the attractive, elastic edge of the thumb method cast-on. You may also see this referred to as the long-tail, or double cast-on, method.

Any style of knitter can use this technique, but it is commonly used by Continental-style knitters, who find the thumb method difficult. It is a little tricky to master, but once you have got the hang of it, it can be quicker to create the cast-on edge than with the thumb method.

As with the thumb method, when you make the initial slip knot, you need to leave a tail of yarn from the loose end of the ball of yarn that is approximately five times as long as your desired cast-on edge. For example, if your piece of knitting is going to be 4 in./10 cm wide, then you need to leave a tail of yarn about 20 in./50 cm long.

You use only one needle with this cast-on technique—but the fingers of the left hand do all the work with the yarn, with the right hand holding the needle.

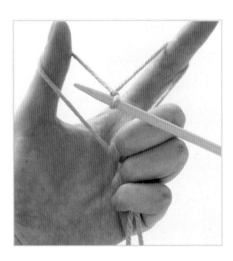

1 Make a slip knot, leaving a tail of yarn roughly five times the width of the cast-on edge. This is something that you will get better at judging with practice. Slip the slip knot onto a needle in your right hand and pull to tighten it to the right size.

2 Grab both ends of yarn in your left hand, with the long tail on the left and the ball end on the right. Insert your thumb and forefinger between the two ends and pull them apart in a diamond shape, as shown in the photo.

3 Pull the needle downward with your right hand, creating a heart shape with the two ends.

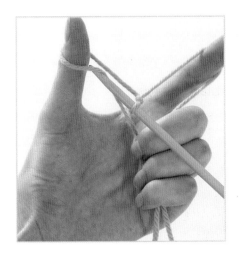

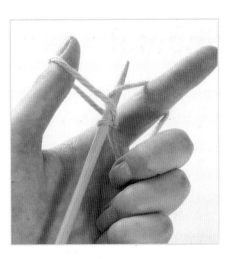

4 Bring the tip of the needle in your right hand up from underneath the bottom of the loop on your left thumb.

5 Insert the needle through the loop of yarn around your thumb and bring it across to the loop on your forefinger, grabbing the yarn from the top of the finger loop with the needle.

6 Draw the loop from your finger down through the thumb loop to create a stitch on the needle.

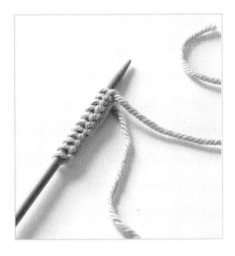

7 Drop the loop from your thumb, keeping all ends taut. With your thumb (or your forefinger and thumb), pull the left-hand end of the yarn to tighten the loop on the needle.

8 Repeat Steps 2–7 until you have cast on the correct number of stitches. The final cast-on edge should look like this.

casting on: two-needle method

The two-needle, or cable, method of casting on is used in the projects in this book
when you have to increase by many stitches at the end of a row or by only a few, as in
the second row of a buttonhole.

For this cast-on, you use both needles—one in each hand, as
when you are knitting. The tail of yarn left before the slip knot
needs to be only long enough to weave it in at the end—
about 6–8 in./15–20 cm long.

The cast-on edge created with this technique is firmer and less
elastic than that produced using either the thumb or the
Continental method, resulting in an edge that is suitable for
more delicate yarns or for items that need extra durability,
such as socks. However, it is not so suitable for edgings that
need extra stretch, such as on hats or cuffs.

The tightness of this cast-on means that you may find it more
difficult to knit into the stitches formed when you begin the
first row of knitting—so make a conscious effort to form each
stitch as loosely as possible.

1 Make a slip knot, ensuring that you leave a
tail long enough to weave in. Slip the knot onto
the needle in your left hand and pull to tighten it.

2 Holding the ball end of the yarn in your right
hand, insert the right-hand needle from front to
back into the loop.

3 With your right hand, wrap the ball end of
the yarn around the needle, passing the yarn first
underneath and then over the needle point.

4   Using the tip of the right-hand needle, draw the yarn looped over the needle through the original slip knot. You should now have one loop on each needle.

5   Place the new loop on the right-hand needle onto the left-hand needle to create a second stitch. Pull gently on the ball end of the yarn to tighten and neaten the stitch.

6   Your first cast-on stitch is complete. Together with the slip knot formed in Step 1, you now have two stitches on the needle.

7   For the next stitch, place the needle from front to back between the two previous stitches. Repeat from Step 3, wrapping the yarn around the needle, but drawing the loop through between the two stitches before placing it on the left-hand needle.

8   Repeat the process until you have the correct number of stitches on the left-hand needle.

garter stitch

knit stitch

Knitting every row forms the ridged fabric called garter stitch (shown on the left). The fabric looks the same on both sides.

1 Hold the needle with the stitches in your left hand. Insert the right-hand needle into the first stitch on the left-hand needle from left to right and front to back.

english method

In the English method of working knit stitch, you hold the needle with the stitches on in your left hand and transfer them all to the right-hand needle by knitting a row. The yarn is held in your right hand and looped around the right-hand needle. You can work more efficiently and quickly by flicking the yarn around the needle with the forefinger of your right hand, so that you do not need to let go of the right-hand needle in the process.

2 Holding the yarn at the back of the work, with your right hand wrap the ball end of the yarn around the right-hand needle, passing the yarn underneath and then over the point.

3 Using the tip of the right-hand needle, draw the yarn looped over the needle through the stitch on the left-hand needle.

4 Keeping the new loop on the right-hand needle, slip the first stitch off the left-hand needle. Repeat these steps until all the stitches are transferred onto the right-hand needle. This completes a knit row. Swap the needles in your hands and start the next row.

continental method

There is a lot of debate about whether the English or the Continental method of knitting is more efficient. Both styles have their plus points, however, so it may be worth experimenting to find out which suits you better.

With the Continental method, the aims are exactly the same as with the English method—namely, to transfer all the stitches from the left-hand needle to the empty right-hand needle. The major difference is that the yarn is held in the left hand. The yarn is then looped around the right-hand needle in the same direction, but this is achieved by a technique known as "picking." Here, the needle does all the work in wrapping, while the left hand holds the yarn very taut to make it easier for the right-hand needle to form the loop.

1 Hold the needle with the stitches in your left hand, with the yarn taut over your left forefinger at the back of the work. Insert the tip of the empty needle into the first stitch of the left-hand needle from left to right and from front to back.

2 Catch the yarn held over your left forefinger by moving the right-hand needle from right to left behind the yarn.

3 Scoop up the yarn with the right-hand needle and draw it through the loop on the left-hand needle.

4 Keeping the newly made loop on the right-hand needle, drop off the loop from the left-hand needle. Repeat until all stitches have been transferred to the right-hand needle. Swap the needles over, so that the empty needle is in your right hand, and begin again for the next row.

stockinette (stocking) stitch

purl stitch

Working alternate rows of knit and purl stitches forms stockinette (stocking) stitch (see photo, left). The side of the fabric shown here is the right side, formed of stitches that look like a "V."

english method

A purl stitch is effectively the opposite of a knit stitch, with the needle inserted the opposite way into each stitch and the yarn held at the front of the work. If you feel more comfortable holding your yarn at the back of the work, you can do so—but make sure that the yarn is still coming from the front, in front of the right-hand needle, and does not twist around the needle while doing so, as this will create an extra stitch.

1 Hold the needle with the stitches on in your left hand. Insert the right-hand needle through the front of the first stitch on the left-hand needle from right to left.

2 Holding the yarn at the back of the work, with your right hand wrap the ball end of the yarn around the right-hand needle, passing the yarn over and around the point.

3 Using the tip of the right-hand needle, draw the yarn looped over the needle back through the stitch on the left-hand needle.

4 Keeping the loop on the right-hand needle, slip the first stitch off the left-hand needle. Repeat until all the stitches are on the right-hand needle. This completes a purl row. Swap the needles in your hands and start a knit row to work stockinette (stocking) stitch.

continental method

With Continental-style purl stitch, there is very little difference in the action from a knit stitch, so many people consider it a much quicker way to purl. The important thing to remember is that, although the yarn is still held in the left hand at the back of the work, you have to ensure that the yarn comes originally from the front of the work, as shown in Step 1. The left forefinger controls the yarn; try to keep the yarn reasonably taut, so that you maintain an even working tension.

If you work every row in purl, it will look exactly the same as garter stitch (see page 22). However, if you want to create a garter-stitch effect, it is easier and quicker to knit every row than to purl them.

Working purl stitch the Continental way can be a little tricky: the yarn is almost parallel to the right needle (Step 1), so it can be hard to wrap the yarn around the right way and it may slip off the needle. Keep the yarn as tight as possible, wrapping it as shown in Step 2.

1 Hold the yarn with the stitches in your left hand. Hold the yarn taut in your left hand, at the front of the work. Insert the right-hand needle from right to left through the front of the first stitch on the left-hand needle.

2 Wrap the right-hand needle underneath and then over the top of the yarn held over your left forefinger, from right to left and then from left to right. Beware of wrapping in the wrong direction—from underneath the needle instead of over the top—as this will cause twisted stitches.

3 Carefully draw the yarn through the loop on the left-hand needle.

4 Keeping the newly made loop on the right-hand needle, drop off the loop from the left-hand needle. Repeat until all the stitches have been transferred to the right-hand needle.

1 x 1 rib stitch

rib stitch

Rib stitch, or ribbing, is used in areas that need to be more elastic, such as cuffs, which need to stretch and then spring back into shape.

Rib stitch is a combination of knit and purl stitches next to each other. These steps demonstrate 1 x 1 rib stitch, which is knit 1, purl 1—abbreviated as "k1, p1"—across the row. The difficulty is keeping track of which stitch you need to work next. Look at Step 2, below left: the next stitch to be worked on the left-hand needle has a bar of yarn across it at the base. This shows that on the previous row it was knitted, so on this row you have to purl it. In Step 4, below right, the next stitch to be worked does not have the bar of yarn, so you must knit it.

1 Here a knit stitch has just been worked, meaning that the yarn is being held at the back of the knitting.

2 To work the next stitch—a purl stitch—the yarn must be at the front of the work. To move it to the correct position, just bring it forward between the needles.

3 Work a purl stitch in the usual way, holding the yarn at the front of the work.

4 Before working the next stitch, a knit stitch, return the yarn between the needles to the back. In the next row, all the stitches that were knitted must be purled and vice versa. So if you end a row with a purl stitch, you must begin the next row with a knit stitch.

variations of rib stitch

Once you have mastered the technique of passing the yarn between the needles
to the other side of the work, you can work any combination of knit and purl stitches
across a row to create other stitch patterns. Ribbing can take many different forms.

2 x 2 rib stitch

A common and attractive version is 2 x 2 rib, shown left. This pattern is formed by knitting two stitches, then purling the following two, and repeating this across the row. It is abbreviated as "k2, p2." This version is popular in garments, as the rib can be more easily seen: 1 x 1 rib, when not at full stretch, can often look like stockinette (stocking) stitch. Once you know how to do 2 x 2 rib, you can experiment with different multiples of knit and purl, such as 3 x 3 or 6 x 6.

seed stitch (also known as moss stitch)

Seed stitch usually uses an odd number of stitches and starts with a 1 x 1 rib stitch (k1, p1) across the row, with the last stitch being knitted. However, unlike 1 x 1 rib, on the next row all the stitches that were knitted must be knitted and those that were purled, purled. This is why an odd number of stitches is helpful, as you know that you will always start and end a row with a knit stitch. Each row will be exactly the same and is written as, "k1, *p1, k1; rep from * to end." If you decide that you have to use an even number of stitches, just remember to keep to the rule of knitting the knits and purling the purls.

fancy ribs

Once you know these simple variations, you can experiment by alternating rib rows with garter or stockinette (stocking) stitch rows.

The coat on page 94 (shown on the left) uses a mixture of 1 x 1 rib and an alternate knit row to create a pretty effect that looks almost woven instead of knitted. It is not as stretchy as a plain rib, but it gives a thicker fabric, which is suitable for outerwear.

shaping knitting

Knitted garments are usually made of shaped pieces, because if you had to cut shapes and sew them together, the edges would be untidy and would unravel. Therefore, shaping must be incorporated as you work.

increasing

To make a piece of knitting wider, you need to increase the number of stitches on the needles. As with casting on, there are several different ways of increasing, but the main differences are purely cosmetic. The method by which you "inc into next st" (shown below) can be used anywhere within a row to obtain different shaping. However, this process can increase only a few stitches at a time, the most common number being just one at a time.

increasing by casting on
This method can be used only at the end of a row, using the two-needle cast-on method, shown on page 20.

inc into next st

1 Insert the right-hand needle into the stitch, wrap the yarn around and draw it through as normal, but do not drop the original stitch off the left-hand needle. Pull the needles apart to make more room in the loop on the left-hand needle.

2 Insert the right-hand needle into the back of the loop on the left-hand needle, from front to back. Wrap the yarn around it with your right hand as if you were knitting normally and draw a second loop through onto the right-hand needle.

3 Now drop the original stitch off the left-hand needle to complete the increase. Two stitches have been made from the one original stitch, so one stitch has been increased.

decreasing

As with increasing, there are different decrease techniques. Here I have shown two of the most common. The difference between the two lies in the direction in which they slant. Knit two together ("k2tog") slants to the right on a knit row, while slip one, knit one, pass slipped stitch over ("sl 1, k1, psso") slants to the left. You can use them at opposite ends of the same row to create a decorative edge. Both these techniques can decrease only a few stitches at a time. If you need to decrease more stitches at the start or end of a row you will have to bind (cast) them off using the basic method shown on page 30.

k2tog

1 Knit to the position of the decrease; here it is being worked at the start of a row. Insert the right-hand needle through the front loops of the next two stitches from front to back.

2 Wrap the yarn around the right-hand needle as usual, and then knit the two stitches as if they were one. One stitch has been decreased.

sl 1, k1, psso

1 Knit to the position of the decrease; here it is being worked at the start of a row. Insert the right-hand needle into the stitch purlwise (from right to left), then slip it from the left-hand needle onto the right-hand needle, without knitting it.

2 Knit the next stitch from the left-hand to the right-hand needle, as usual.

3 Using the tip of the left-hand needle, lift the first (slipped) stitch on the right-hand needle over the second (knitted) stitch and then drop it right off the right-hand needle, thus leaving only one stitch on the right-hand needle. One stitch has been decreased.

binding (casting) off: basic method

Binding (casting) off finishes the edge of a piece of knitting so that the stitches do not unravel when you remove it from the needles.

Binding (casting) off uses both needles. It is easy to make the edge too tight, which would gather in the top of your fabric and place it under extra strain. Keep the stitches loose, or bind (cast) off using needles slightly larger than those used for the rest of the fabric.

1 Knit the first two stitches from the left-hand to the right-hand needle, as normal.

2 Insert the tip of the left-hand needle into the first stitch on the right-hand needle.

3 Pull the first stitch up and lift it over the second stitch.

4 Drop the first stitch off the right-hand needle so that only one stitch remains. Knit the next stitch from the left-hand needle; once again, you will have two stitches on the right-hand needle. Repeat from Step 2, until there is just one stitch on the right-hand needle.

5 Pull on the right-hand needle to increase the size of the last stitch to a large loop. Remove the needle and cut the yarn, leaving a 6–8-in./ 15–20-cm tail. Slip the cut end of the yarn through the loop. Pull on the yarn end to tighten the loop into a knot and secure the edge.

binding (casting) off: seam method

Sometimes it is easier and neater to finish an edge and seam two edges together at the same time, especially when knitting with double-pointed needles. This method, which uses three needles, is often used for shoulder seams, where the stitches have been left on stitch holders and each edge has the same number of stitches.

This method saves both time and yarn, as you do not need to bind (cast) off twice and then sew the seams together; instead, you can carry out all three processes in one step, at the same time. It can look neater than some sewn seams, especially at the shoulders. It is also used for items such as socks (see page 120) where, for reasons of comfort, it is important to have a less bulky seam.

If you are using three straight needles instead of double-pointed needles (typically on shoulder seams), make sure the two needles holding the stitches point in the same direction. If you do not have three straight needles the same size, hold the stitches on two smaller needles, or on stitch holders, and use a larger needle to knit from and bind (cast) off. This will also help prevent the seam from becoming too tight.

1 Hold each needle with the edge stitches aligning and the right sides of the work facing each other. Insert the tip of a third needle through the first stitch on the front and back needles at the same time. Wrap yarn around the third needle, as when working normal knit stitch.

2 Finish the knit stitch by drawing the loop through both front and back stitches.

3 Drop first loops off front and back working needles, leaving one stitch on right-hand needle. Repeat Steps 1–3 with the second stitch of each needle, giving two stitches on right-hand needle. Pass the first stitch on right-hand needle over the second. Continue until seam is complete.

knitting in the round

Knitting in the round is a method of knitting that creates a seamless fabric. It is done using either a circular needle or a set of four or five double-pointed needles (dpns). The technique is particularly useful for working neckbands and socks.

The photographs below demonstrate knitting in the round using a set of four dpns, with the cast-on stitches spread evenly over three needles to start. If you are using a circular knitting needle, spread all the stitches out over the length of the cable and place a stitch marker on the needle in between the first and last stitch to denote the beginning of the round.

When knitting in the round, you never turn the fabric as you would when working in rows. The same side of the knitting is always facing you. When you are working stockinette (stocking) stitch in the round, you never need to purl: simply knit every row. In garter stitch (where you usually knit every row) you need to alternate between knit and purl rounds.

Before you begin knitting, make sure the cast-on stitches are not twisted. An easy way to do this is to check that the bottom edge of the cast-on of each needle is pointing inward, as in Step 1, below.

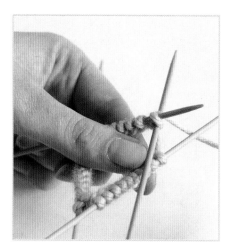

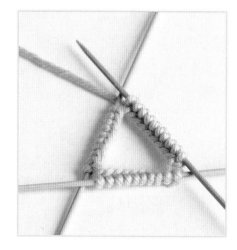

1 Cast the required number of stitches onto one dpn, then separate the stitches evenly over three or four needles, depending on the length of cast-on. Arrange the needles in a triangular shape, taking care to ensure that the stitches are not twisted.

2 Insert the empty dpn knitwise into the first cast-on stitch. Wrap the tail of yarn from the cast-on around the needle to complete the stitch. Pull tight to close the gap. When all stitches from first dpn have been knitted, knit the stitches off the next dpn onto the empty needle.

3 One round completed. Note that the stitches on each needle are pulled up tightly to those on the adjoining needle, in order to prevent gapping in the final fabric.

cable knitting

Cables are stitches that look like twisted ropes and braids (plaits). Making a cable involves working a stitch, or group of stitches, out of sequence. A cable needle is used to hold the first stitch(es) to the front or back while you work the following stitch(es); then the stitches on the cable needle are worked.

In patterns, basic cable abbreviations begin with a capital letter "C" (for "cable"), followed by an even number (usually) that denotes the number of stitches over which the cable will be worked. These stitches are then split into two, and are worked out of sequence. For example, when you are cabling over four stitches, the sequence in which the stitches will be knitted will be 3, 4, 1, 2.

A capital letter "B" or "F" after the number denotes whether the cable needle is to be held at the back or front of the work. This determines the direction of twist of the cable. C4B means that the cable will be over four stitches and that the cable needle will be held at the back of the work, creating a right-leaning or "Z" twist. C4F will create a left-leaning or "S" twist, as the stitches on the cable needle are held at the front.

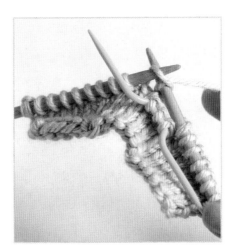

1 The cable being demonstrated is C6F—in other words, the next 6 stitches will be cabled to the front. Work in pattern to position of the 6 cable stitches. Slip the next 3 stitches onto the cable needle and hold at the front of work.

2 Ignoring the stitches on the cable needle, knit the next 3 stitches from the left-hand needle.

3 Once these 3 stitches have been knitted, slip the 3 stitches on the cable needle to the right-hand end of needle and knit these 3 stitches from the cable needle. Put down the cable needle until it is needed again.

other useful techniques

The following techniques are simple to master and will provide professional-looking touches on your knitting.

joining in new yarn

When you have run out of yarn, you must join in a new ball. Try to do this at the beginning of a row, as the join will be much neater than in the middle of a row. Insert the right-hand needle into the next stitch, as usual. Leaving a 6–8-in./15–20-cm tail, loop the end of the new yarn over the tip of the right-hand needle, draw it through, and drop the original stitch. You have made one stitch with the new yarn. Knit the next few stitches as usual, then gently pull the first stitch taut and tie the two ends of yarn in a loose knot to secure them.

You can use the same technique to join in a different color of yarn—when working in stripes, for example. With stripes, however, you do not have to cut off the yarn and tie in a new color every time. Instead, you can carry the color that you are not using loosely up the edge of the work, twisting it with the other color at the end of the row until you need to use it again. However, this twisting technique can begin to look untidy on wide stripes. If the edge will not be hidden in a seam, it may be better to join in new yarn each time you begin a new stripe and then weave in the loose ends (see page 36) at the end.

knitting stitches for edges

Sometimes you have to pick up some stitches from the edge of a completed piece of knitted fabric in order to knit another part of the project. The pattern will tell you where on the knitted fabric you need to pick up from. Follow the steps shown on the right, then just knit the stitches following the pattern instructions. Weave in the loose end of yarn neatly (see page 36) when the knitting is complete.

1 With right side facing you, insert the needle through the middle of first stitch to be picked up, from front to back. Wrap the yarn around the needle at the back of the fabric, as if to knit, and pull the loop through to the front of the fabric.

2 Repeat in the next stitch along, or as often as instructed in your pattern, picking up stitches evenly along the edge until you have the required number of stitches.

1 On a knit row, knit to the position of the buttonhole. Bind (cast) off the number of stitches stated in the pattern, or enough to accommodate the button you want to use. Continue knitting to the end of the row.

2 Purl to the buttonhole. Turn the work around and cast on the same number of stitches as were bound (cast) off in the previous row. Turn the work back and purl on the other side of the buttonhole to the end of the row. Buttonhole complete.

buttonholes

Buttonholes can be worked quite easily within knitting by binding (casting) off a certain number of stitches on one row, then casting them on again in the next. When making buttonholes, use the two-needle method of casting on along the edge for neatness and durability (see page 20).

1 Knit to the position of the eyelet. Bring the yarn between the needles to the front (yo), then knit the next two stitches together (k2tog). This cancels out the increase made by bringing the yarn over. On the next row knit the yarn-over loop as if it were a normal stitch.

2 To make lace patterns, continue to work eyelet holes as in Step 1 (yo, k2tog), at even intervals across the row. Here you can see how the gaps are evident even as you are knitting the row. Knit or purl the next row in the normal way before working more eyelets.

eyelets/laceholes

The eyelet hole is easy to create and is commonly used to make small buttonholes in clothes for babies and young children.

If you work eyelets throughout a piece of knitting a lace effect is achieved. At its simplest, lace knitting is making planned holes at regular intervals. It is basically a series of eyelet holes arranged to create a pattern—but with each eyelet, which is in effect an increase (yo), there is a corresponding decrease (k2tog) to ensure that the pattern keeps a constant number of stitches. The pattern or chart for the lace piece will always show you where to increase and decrease.

finishing

The finishing of a garment is often something knitters dread, as bad finishing is glaringly obvious. However, if you learn to do it correctly, finishing is very satisfying.

weaving in ends

Never, ever cut the loose ends of yarn left at the edges of your knitting to less than 6–8 in./15–20 cm long, or they may slip through the stitches and unravel. Untie the knots holding two ends of yarn together before weaving in the ends. Thread a large-eyed tapestry, or yarn, needle with the tail of yarn, and follow one of the methods shown below to weave the tail into the back of the knitted fabric. The needle needs to be blunt so that the point does not pass through the strands of yarn, which can become messy.

blocking

Blocking involves pinning out your knitted pieces to their finished measurements and then setting the fabric shape by pressing with an iron. It is important to block pieces before you sew them up, for many reasons. If the pieces have knit up unevenly or are slightly too small, inventive blocking can work wonders by manipulating them gently into shape. Blocking also sets the stitches and yarn, enhancing the fabric's drape, and can subdue curling in stockinette (stocking) stitch slightly, allowing for easier sewing up of the edges.

method 1

Thread the needle and yarn through the loops along the edge of the work for about 2–3 in./5–7 cm, then sew back through a few of the last loops to secure the yarn.

method 2

Thread the needle and yarn through the stitches, inserting the needle through the top of the loop on the first stitch and then through the bottom on the next for about 2–3 in./5–7 cm along. Sew back through a few of the last loops to secure.

blocking

Before you sew up a garment, block the pieces to get the best possible finish. Lay the piece on a padded surface such as an ironing board, and pin it flat, easing it gently into the right shape. Press it, following the instructions on the label.

sewing seams

Mattress stitch, which is done using a tapestry (yarn) needle, is the best way to join seams. In a stockinette (stocking) stitch or ribbed fabric, mattress stitch is invisible if worked correctly, as you can see at the bottom of the seam being sewn in the photo below. Always use the same color yarn as in the main body of work so that the joining yarn cannot be seen (here, a contrasting color has been used for clarity). Some yarns may be too weak to sew up a seam, so double these up, or add a stronger yarn to the original one, or use a different yarn altogether, but make sure it is a similar color.

reinforcing for snap fasteners

With a child's garment it is absolutely essential that you sew on any buttons or snap fasteners securely, so that there is no risk of them working loose and become a choking hazard. Due to the stretchy nature of knitted fabric, any area to which snap fasteners are to be attached should be reinforced so that the action of fastening the garment does not pull it out of shape or rip the yarn. You can do this by sewing the snap fasteners to a length of grosgrain (petersham) ribbon or bias tape and then sewing this tape to the garment, taking care to ensure that it is concealed from view.

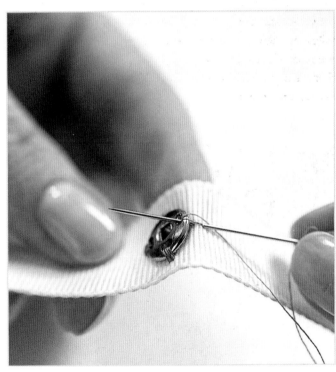

mattress stitch

With right sides upward, secure the yarn on the back of one piece. Bring the needle to the front, between the edge stitch and the next stitch in. Take the needle across to the other piece and pick up two loops between the edge stitch and the next stitch, as shown above. Pull the yarn through and pull taut. Take the needle back to the first piece, insert it where it exited, and pick up two loops. Continue, going from one side to the other, until you reach the last stitch. Secure the yarn on the back with a few small stitches.

reinforcing for snap fasteners

Using a sewing needle and thread, stitch the snaps firmly to a piece of grosgrain (petersham) ribbon or bias tape. Using the same needle and thread and overcasting (over-sewing) stitches, neatly sew the ribbon or tape to the back of the garment where the fastening needs to be.

gauge (tension)

A gauge (tension) swatch is used to check that you are knitting to the gauge (tension) called for in the pattern. This is essential in order to ensure that you knit the garment to the right size, so do take the time to knit a swatch before you embark on a project.

there are fewer stitches than required, then your working tension is too loose; try again with smaller needles.

Don't worry if your gauge (tension) is not correct first time. Knitting is not a precise art and knitters vary widely in their working tension. For projects where a good fit is not required, such as some accessories and toys, you do not need to complete a swatch—unless you want to make sure that the size is as stated on the pattern. If you will be using the same yarn again in another project, label your swatch and store it for future reference. If you are worried about wasting yarn with a gauge (tension) swatch, unravel it to use the yarn in the garment.

To work a gauge (tension) swatch, knit a square about 5 x 5 in./12.5 x 12.5 cm, using the needles, yarn, and stitch pattern stated in the gauge instructions. Lay the swatch flat and, keeping away from the edges, measure and mark out 4 in. (10 cm) with marker pins. Count the number of stitches between the pins. Then repeat the process in the other direction to count the number of rows.

Your pattern will tell you how many rows and how many stitches there should be in 4 square inches (10 square centimeters) over a given stitch. If you find you have more stitches than required, then your gauge is too tight. Don't try to knit more loosely, as everyone has a natural tension (degree of control when knitting), and you won't be able to keep your stitches consistent. Instead, try again with bigger needles. If

counting rows

It is easy to lose track of which row you are on while knitting, but it is just as easy to count the rows already worked.

In garter stitch (in which each row is knit), each ridge is two rows, so count each of these ridges and multiply by two to reach the number of rows. In stockinette (stocking) stitch, each "V" shape is one stitch—so if you count up a vertical row of "V"s, you will know how many rows you have worked. Alternatively, count the ridges on the purl side.

Remember that the cast-on is not counted as a row—and, if you are counting rows while you are still in the process of knitting, you also need to count the stitches that are on your needle as the last row.

fixing mistakes

There are many mistakes to be made in knitting, and it is odd how beginners frequently make the same ones. Gaining or losing stitches is the most common error.

When knitting straight, beginners often end up with slanting edges caused by either gaining or losing stitches.

To avid gaining stitches, count your stitches at the start of every row as you work to see if you can spot where the mistake has been made. Be careful not to pass the yarn from front to back when it is not called for, do not wrap the yarn twice around the needle when knitting, and always remember to drop the final loop at the end of a stitch. The best thing to do when learning is to take it very slowly and try not to get distracted. By counting the stitches at the beginning of a row, you will

ideally avoid the common beginner's mistake of counting the first stitch as two; because the edge stitches can be quite loose when you are inexperienced, they can often be twisted and look like two separate stitches.

It is inevitable as a beginner that you will drop stitches, but luckily dropped stitches are nearly as easy to fix as they are to make. The steps below show how to pick up a dropped stitch with your knitting needles. Once you have mastered the principle, try doing this with a small crochet hook, as it is quicker and easier when you know how.

1 This picture shows what a dropped stitch looks like. If left, it will drop farther down the rows to form a run (ladder). If this occurs you must pick up each strand of the run, from lowest first, to account for each row.

2 Firstly, slip the dropped stitch loop onto the right-hand needle. With the tip of the same needle, pick up the lowest strand of yarn in the run, taking the needle under the strand from front to back.

3 Slip the stitch loop over the strand and off the right-hand needle. The strand has become the new stitch loop. Continue until all the strands in the run have been picked up. Slip the final stitch loop onto the left-hand needle.

reading patterns

At first glance, patterns can seem as if they are written in a foreign language, as they are composed mainly of abbreviations. If you know what each one is short for, however, you can read the pattern as you would an ordinary piece of writing. Always go through a new pattern first, to make sure you understand all the abbreviations and techniques.

A list of the abbreviations used in this book is given opposite. The most important abbreviations are "k" for knit and "p" for purl. These abbreviations are generally next to a number that indicates how many stitches need to be knitted or purled. For example, "k2" means "knit two stitches."

The other important symbols to watch for are commas, asterisks, and brackets. Commas separate single instructions; for example, "k1, p2" means "knit one stitch, purl the next two stitches." Asterisks indicate a section in a pattern that is repeated more than once; the number of repetitions will be specified farther along in the row. For example, "k1, *p1, k1; rep from * to end" means "knit the first stitch, then purl and knit alternate stitches until you reach the end of the row."

Square brackets enclose instructions that need to be worked a number of times, with the number of times written immediately after the closing bracket. For example, "[k1, p2] 8 times" means, "knit one stitch, then purl two stitches, and repeat this sequence eight times in total." Parentheses (round brackets) indicate different sizes; the smallest size is listed first, before the opening parenthesis, then come all the other sizes in parentheses, with the largest size last. Where there are many different sizes you may find it helpful to circle with a pencil all the instructions for your particular size before you start knitting. Numbers in italics at the end of a row are the stitch count—the number of stitches you should have after finishing the row. Again, numbers in parentheses are for larger sizes.

sizing

Throughout this book, the sizing for a project is given at the start of the pattern. We have used an average size for each age and have given the actual measurements of the finished garment underneath. This allows you to choose the size of the garment you want to make by comparing its finished size with the size of the child it is for. In this way, even if you have a taller, lighter, or smaller than average child, you can make a garment that will fit them—or one that they can grow into.

Even if you are making the garment for the child to wear now, remember to allow some room for movement: don't knit the chest size that is exactly the child's measurement. Also, take the time to get your gauge (tension) right (see page 38), so that the finished garment will be as close as possible to the size you want.

Many of the patterns also indicate where you can adapt the length of the body or arms by knitting more or fewer rows. This is especially helpful if your child is particularly tall or short for his or her age.

abbreviations

alt	alternate		stitch over
beg	beginning	rem	remaining
cont	continue	rep	repeat
dec	decrease	RS	right side
DK	double knitting	sl	slip
dpn	double-pointed	st(s)	stitch(es)
	needle	st-st	stockinette
foll	following		(stocking) stitch
inc	increase	tbl	through the
k	knit		back of loop
m	make (a stitch)		(of a stitch)
p	purl	tog	together
patt	pattern	WS	wrong side
PM	place marker	yo	yarn over
psso	pass slipped		

clothes

stripy sweater

Working in wide stripes is an extremely effective way of making a simple crew-neck sweater look more interesting. This design uses rainbow shades, with red as a bold edging on the neck and cuffs for a sophisticated finish.

materials

2 (3: 3: 3: 3) x 2 oz/50 g balls of Debbie Bliss Baby Cashmerino in shade 23, (red, yarn A), 55% merino wool, 33% microfiber, 12% cashmere, 120 yd/110 m

1 (2: 2: 2: 2) x 2 oz/50 g balls of Debbie Bliss Baby Cashmerino in shade 17 (yellow, yarn B), 55% merino wool, 33% microfiber, 12% cashmere, 120 yd/110 m

1 (2: 2: 2: 2) x 2 oz/50 g balls of Debbie Bliss Baby Cashmerino in shade 503 (green, yarn C), 55% merino wool, 33% microfiber, 12% cashmere, 120 yd/110 m

1 (2: 2: 2: 2) x 2 oz/50 g balls of Debbie Bliss Baby Cashmerino in shade 203 (blue, yarn D), 55% merino wool, 33% microfiber, 12% cashmere, 120 yd/110 m

1 (2: 2: 2: 2) x 2 oz/50 g balls of Debbie Bliss Baby Cashmerino in shade 13 (mauve, yarn E), 55% merino wool, 33% microfiber, 12% cashmere, 120 yd/110 m

Pair of size 2 (3 mm) knitting needles

Pair of size 3 (3.25 mm) knitting needles

Stitch holders

Tapestry (yarn) needle

gauge (tension)

24 sts and 35 rows to 4 in./10 cm over st st on size 3 (3.25 mm) needles. Always check gauge (tension) carefully, and adjust needle size if necessary (see page 38).

measurements

TO FIT CHEST SIZE	22 in./56 cm	23½ in./60 cm	25 in./64 cm	26¾ in./68 cm	28¼ in./72 cm
ACTUAL CHEST SIZE	24¾ in./63 cm	27½ in./70 cm	28¾ in./73 cm	30 in./76 cm	31½ in./80 cm
ACTUAL BACK LENGTH	12¼ in./31 cm	14 in./35.5 cm	15½ in./39.5 cm	16½ in./41.5 cm	18 in./45.5 cm
UNDERARM SLEEVE LENGTH	11½ in./29 cm	12½ in./32 cm	13½ in./34 cm	14¼ in./36 cm	15 in./38 cm

Work straight on these 60 (64: 68: 72: 72) sts until work measures 12 (13½: 15: 15¾: 17¾) in./30 (34: 38: 40: 44) cm from cast-on edge, ending with a purl row.

shape shoulders

Bind (cast) off 6 (3: 4: 5: 5) sts at beg of next 2 rows, then bind (cast) off 6 (5: 5: 5: 5) sts on at beg of foll 2 (4: 4: 4: 4) rows, place rem 36 (38: 40: 42: 42) sts on holder.

front

Work as for Back between ** and **.
Maintaining continuity of stripe sequence, work straight on these 60 (64: 68: 72: 72) sts until work measures 10¼ (12: 13½: 14¼: 15¾) in./26 (30: 34: 36: 40) cm from cast-on edge, ending with a purl row.

divide for neck

K22 (23: 24: 25: 25), turn, leaving rem 38 (41: 44: 47: 47) sts on holder.
Work on these 22 (23: 24: 25: 25) sts for left neck as folls:
Dec 1 st at neck edge every row until 14 (15: 16: 17: 17) sts rem, then dec 1 st at neck edge on every alt row until 12 (13: 14: 15: 15) sts rem, then work straight until Front measures same as Back to start of shoulder shaping, ending with a purl row. Shape left shoulder as folls:
Bind (cast) off 6 (3: 4: 5: 5) sts at beg of next row, then 6 (5: 5: 5: 5) sts at beg of foll 1 (2: 2: 2: 2) alt rows.
Attach yarn to rem 38 (41: 44: 48: 48) sts, k across 16 (18: 20: 22: 22) sts, place these 16 (18: 20: 22: 22) sts on a holder, k to end of row.
Work on these 22 (23: 24: 25: 25) sts for right neck as folls:
Dec 1 st at neck edge of every row until 14 (15: 16: 17: 17) sts rem, then dec 1 st at neck edge of every alt row until 12 (13: 14: 15: 15) sts rem, then work straight until Front measures same as Back to start of shoulder shaping, ending with a knit row. Shape shoulder as folls:
Bind (cast) off 6 (3: 4: 5: 5) sts at beg of next row, then 6 (5: 5: 5: 5) sts at beg of foll 1 (2: 2: 2: 2) alt rows.

back

**Using size 2 (3 mm) needles and yarn A, cast on 76 (84: 88: 92: 96) sts.
Work 10 rows in 2 x 2 rib as folls: [k2, p2] across every row.
Change to yarn B and size 3 (3.25 mm) needles.
Beg with a knit row, work straight in st st in stripes until Back measures 6½ (7¾: 9: 9½: 11) in./16 (20: 23: 24: 28) cm from cast-on edge, or desired length, ending with a purl row, as folls: 6 rows of each color in sequence B, C, D, E, A.

shape armholes

Bind (cast) off 3 (4: 4: 4: 5) sts at beg of next 2 rows, then dec 1 st at each end of next 3 rows and foll 2 (3: 3: 3: 4) alt rows. *60 (64: 68: 72: 72) sts**

sleeves (make two alike)

Using size 2 (3 mm) needles and yarn A, cast on 40 (44: 44: 48: 52) sts.

Work 10 rows in 2 x 2 rib as folls: [k2, p2] across every row.

Change to yarn B and size 3 (3.25 mm) needles.

(Throughout rest of Sleeve, work in st st in stripes as folls: 6 rows of each color in sequence B, C, D, E, A.)

Beg with a knit row, work 4 rows straight in st st.

Maintaining continuity of stripe pattern, as for Back, inc 1 st at each end of next and every foll 5th (6th: 6th: 6th: 7th) row until there are 72 (74: 78: 82: 84) sts.

Cont in st st without increasing until sleeve measures 11½ (12½: 13½: 14¼: 15) in./29 (32: 34: 36: 38) cm from cast-on edge, ending with a purl row.

shape sleeve top

Bind (cast) off 3 (4: 4: 4: 5) sts at beg of next 2 rows, then dec 1 st at each end of next 3 rows and foll 2 (3: 3: 3: 4) alt rows. *56 (54: 58: 62: 60) sts*

Bind (cast) off all sleeve sts.

to finish

Block and press all pieces.

Using mattress stitch, sew right shoulder seam.

Attach yarn A to left front neck. Using size 2 (3 mm) needles and with RS facing, pick up and knit 16 (18: 18: 20: 20) sts down left neck, knit 16 (18: 20: 22: 22) sts from center neck holder, pick up and knit 16 (18: 18: 20: 20) sts up right front neck, then knit 36 (38: 40: 42: 42) sts from back neck stitch holder. *84 (92: 96: 104: 104) sts*

Turn and work 1 row in 2 x 2 rib.

Work 5 more rows in 2 x 2 rib, then bind (cast) off very loosely in rib.

Sew left shoulder seam and neck seam.

Fold sleeves in half lengthwise. Matching center top of sleeve to shoulder seam, using mattress stitch, sew bound-off (cast-off) edge of sleeve to edge of main body, then sew side and underarm seams in one long seam on each side.

To complete the sweater, carefully weave in all the loose ends of yarn.

ribbon-trimmed shrug

This simple shrug is effectively a long piece of knitting folded and sewn up at the cuffs, with an edging then knitted on. The edging is knitted in the round, which might seem a little tricky to begin with, but once you have got the hang of joining the work, you'll find that knitting in the round is quick and easy—just like this pattern! The holes made for threading the ribbon disappear into the ribbing, so the garment works just as well without the ribbon for everyday wear. The bamboo yarn used here has a beautiful heavy drape, which you may wish to take into consideration if substituting a different yarn; a cotton double knitting (DK) yarn might create this drape just as well.

materials
3 (4: 4) x 2 oz/50 g balls of Sirdar Snuggly Baby Bamboo
   in shade 148, 80% bamboo, 20% wool, 105 yd/94 m,
Pair of size 6 (4 mm) knitting needles
Pair of size 4 (3.5 mm) knitting needles
Size 4 (3.5 mm) circular knitting needles
60-in./150-cm length of ¼-in./5-mm ribbon
Tapestry (yarn) needle

gauge (tension)
22 sts and 28 rows to 4 in./10 cm over st st on size 6 (4mm) needles. Always check gauge (tension) carefully, and adjust needle size if necessary (see page 38).

measurements
S (M: L), to fit chest up to 23½ (26: 28¾) in./60 (66: 73) cm.

note
Make sure that you cast on and bind (cast) off very loosely for this pattern, as the ribbing will be around the widest part of the arm. I recommend the thumb or Continental methods (see page 18), which are loose cast-ons ideal for ribbing.

shrug

Using size 4 (3.5 mm) needles, cast on 38 (46: 50) sts.

Work in 2 x 2 rib as folls:

Row 1: K2, *p2, k2, rep from * to end.

Row 2: P2, *k2, p2, rep from * to end.

Rep these two rows until work measures 4 in./10 cm, ending with a Row 2.

Change to size 6 (4 mm) needles.

small and medium sizes only

Next row: Knit to end.

Starting with a purl row, work 17½ (18½) in./44 (47) cm in st st, ending with a purl row.

large size only

Next row: Inc in first st, k15, inc in next st, k16, inc in next st, k to last st, inc in last st. *54 sts*

Starting with a purl row, work 19¾ in./50 cm in st st, ending with a purl row as folls:

Last row: P2tog, p15, p2tog, p16, p2tog, p to last 2 sts, p2tog. *50 sts*

all sizes

Change to size 4 (3.5 mm) needles and work 4 in./10 cm in 2 x 2 rib as before.

Bind (cast) off all sts.

Work measures 25 (25½: 27½) in./64 (67: 70) cm in total.

edging

With the right (knit) side showing, fold work in half lengthwise to form a long, thin tube. Using mattress stitch, sew seams together along ribbing at each end, leaving the st st section free.

These ribbed ends will form the cuffs.

Using a size 4 (3.5 mm) circular needle, with RS facing, pick up and knit 108 (114: 120) sts evenly along bottom edge of st st section, from cuff to cuff, then continue around edge, picking up 108 (114: 120) sts along top edge. When all 216 (228: 240) sts are picked up, the first and last st will meet at one cuff. Join for working in the round (see page 32) and place marker for start of round.

Working in the round, knit one row, increasing and making eyelet holes as folls:

Round 1 (inc round): *K3, yo, rep from * to end of rnd. *288 (304: 320) sts*

Work in 2 x 2 rib as folls:

Round 2: *K2, p2, rep from * to end of rnd.

Rep Round 2 until rib measures 2½ in./6 cm.

Bind (cast) off all sts loosely.

to finish

Weave in all ends.

Thread ribbon through eyelet holes all around edging, tying in a bow if desired. Do not pull the ribbon too tightly through the holes or the fabric may bunch up and distort the final measurements.

v-neck sweater

A simple V-neck sweater is a practical essential in any wardrobe, and this versatile garment can be dressed up with a shirt or worn casually with a T-shirt. The deep ribbed cuffs and raglan sleeves on this pattern are attractive features.

materials

6 (6: 7: 8) x 2 oz/50 g balls of Sublime Cashmere Merino Silk DK in shade 12 (ink), 75% extra fine merino, 20% silk, 5% cashmere, 126 yd/116 m
Pair of size 3 (3.25 mm) knitting needles
Pair of size 6 (4 mm) knitting needles
Tapestry (yarn) needle

gauge (tension)

22 sts and 30 rows to 4 in./10 cm over st st on size 6 (4 mm) needles.

Always check gauge (tension) carefully, and adjust needle size if necessary (see page 38).

measurements

APPROX. CHEST SIZE	22¾ in./58 cm	24¾ in./63 cm	26¾ in./68 cm	28¾ in./73 cm
ACTUAL CHEST SIZE	26¾ in./68 cm	29 in./73.5 cm	31 in./79 cm	33 in./84 cm
ACTUAL BACK LENGTH	13¾ in./35 cm	16 in./40.5 cm	17¾ in./45 cm	18¼ in./46.5 cm
UNDERARM SLEEVE LENGTH	11½ in./29 cm	12½ in./32 cm	14¼ in./36 cm	15 in./38 cm

N.B. Allow extra length on back and arms for a slight overhang at ribbing on cuffs and waist.

back

**Using size 3 (3.25 mm) needles, cast on 75 (81: 87: 93) sts. Work in 1 x 1 rib as folls:
Row 1: K1, *p1, k1, rep from * to end of row.
Row 2: P1, *k1, p1, rep from * to end of row.
Rep these 2 rows until work measures 2¼ (2¾: 2¾: 3¼) in./6 (7: 7: 8) cm from cast-on edge, ending with a Row 2.
Change to size 6 (4 mm) needles.
Cont in st st until work measures 8¼ (9¾: 11: 11½) in./21 (25: 28: 29) cm from cast-on edge, or desired length from hip to underarm to fit your child, ending with a purl row.**

shape armholes

Bind (cast) off 3 (3: 3: 4) sts at beg of next 2 rows, then dec 1 st at each end of next and every foll alt row as folls: K1, sl 1, k1, psso, k to last 3 sts, k2tog, k1 until 27 (29: 31: 33) sts rem.
Leave rem 27 (29: 31: 33) sts on a holder.

front

Work as for Back from ** to **.

shape armholes

Bind (cast) off 3 (3: 3: 4) sts at beg of next 2 rows, then divide for neck as folls:

left neck

Row 1: K1, sl 1, k1, psso, k31 (34: 37: 39), turn, leaving rem 35 (38: 41: 43) sts on holder.
Dec 1 st at neck edge of next row and foll 4 (4: 4: 5) alt rows, then every foll 4th row, and at the same time dec 1 st at armhole edge of this and every foll alt row until 1 st rem. Fasten off rem st.

right neck

Leaving center st on holder, rejoin yarn to neck edge of right neck, with RS facing. K to last 3 sts, k2 tog, k1. Complete neck, matching shaping to mirror left side as folls:
Dec 1 st at neck edge of next row and foll 4 (4: 4: 5) alt rows, every foll 4th row, and at the same time dec 1 st at armhole edge of this and every foll alt row until 1 st rem. Fasten off.

sleeves (make two alike)

Using size 3 (3.25 mm) needles, cast on 33 (35: 37: 39) sts. Work in 1 x 1 rib as folls:
Row 1: K1, *p1, k1, rep from * to end of row.
Row 2: P1, *k1, p1, rep from * to end of row.
Rep these 2 rows until work measures 2¼ (2¾: 2¾: 3¼) in./6 (7: 7: 8) cm from cast-on edge, ending with a Row 2.
Change to size 6 (4 mm) needles and work in st st, inc 1 st at each end of 7th and every foll 6th row until there are 49 (53: 57: 61) sts. Cont in st st until sleeve measures 11½ (12½: 14¼: 15) in./29 (32: 36: 38) cm or desired length from wrist to underarm to fit your child, ending with a purl row.

shape sleeve top

Bind (cast) off 3 (3: 3: 4) sts at beg of next 2 rows, then 1 st at each end of next and every foll alt row as folls: K1, sl 1, k1, psso, k to last 3 sts, k2tog, k1 until 1 st rem. Fasten off rem st.

to finish

Block and press all pieces.
Using mattress stitch, attach front to left sleeve by sewing up raglan sleeve seam. Attach back to left sleeve in same way. Attach back to right sleeve along raglan sleeve seam, but do not attach right sleeve seam to front.
Using size 3 (3.25 mm) needles and with right side facing, join yarn to top of right sleeve. Pick up and knit 1 st from sleeve edge, then knit along 27 (29: 31: 33) sts on holder at neck edge. Pick up and knit 1 st from top of left raglan sleeve, then 38 (40: 42: 44) sts down left front neck, pick up 1 stitch from holder at center v, pick up and knit 38 (40: 42: 44) sts up right front edge. *106 (112: 118: 124) sts*
Turn and work 1 row in 1 x 1 rib.
Work 3 more rows in 1 x 1 rib, then bind (cast) off all sts in rib. Sew up rem raglan seam and rib seam, then sew up side and sleeve seams. Weave in all ends.

swing cardigan

It is easy to change a basic cardigan pattern into a very pretty and stylish piece. This pattern has three-quarter length sleeves and swings out at the waist to create a very feminine line. The yoke is knitted in one piece as a deep ribbed collar; use very long straight needles or, preferably, a long circular one, so that you can fit on all the yoke stitches.

materials
6 (6: 7: 8) x 2 oz/.50 g balls of Sublime Baby Cashmere Merino
   Silk DK in shade 0006 (pebble), 75% extra fine merino, 20%
   silk, 5% cashmere, 127 yd/116 m
Size 6 (4 mm) knitting needles
Stitch holders
Stitch markers
Tapestry (yarn) needle

1 x 1⅛ in./30-mm button
Sewing needle and thread

gauge (tension)
22 sts and 28 rows to 4 in./10 cm over st st on size 6 (4 mm) needles. Always check gauge (tension) carefully, and adjust needle size if necessary (see page 38).

measurements

TO FIT CHEST SIZE	23½ in./60 cm	25 in./64 cm	26¾ in./68 cm	28¼ in./72 cm
ACTUAL CHEST SIZE	25½ in./65 cm	27¼ in./69 cm	28¾ in./73 cm	30 in./76 cm
ACTUAL LENGTH	13 in./33 cm	14½ in./37 cm	15¼ in./39 cm	16½ in./42 cm
UNDERARM LENGTH (¾ LENGTH)	7 in./18 cm	7½ in./19 cm	7¾ in./20 cm	8¼ in./21 cm

back

Using size 6 (4 mm) needles, cast on 86 (92: 96: 102) sts.
Work 1⅛ in./3 cm in garter st (knit every row).
Beg with a purl row, cont in st st, decreasing 1 st at each end
of 2nd row and every foll 6th (6th: 8th: 8th) row until 74 (78:
82: 86) sts rem.
Cont in st st until Back measures 7 (8½: 9½: 10¾) in./18 (22: 24:
27) cm from cast-on edge, or desired length, ending with a
purl row.

shape armholes

Bind (cast) off 3 (4: 4: 5) sts at beg of next 2 rows. *68 (70: 74:
76) sts*
Dec 1 st at each end of foll 4 rows. *60 (62: 66: 68) sts*
Dec 1 st at each end of foll 2 alt rows. *56 (58: 62: 64) sts*
Knit 1 row.
Place these 56 (58: 62: 64) sts on holder.

left front

Using size 6 (4 mm) needles, cast on 48 (52: 54: 58) sts.
Work 1⅛ in./3 cm in garter st (knit every row).
Cont in st st, with a garter st border, dec 1 st at beg of Row
2 and then at non-garter side seam on every foll 6th (6th: 8th:
8th) row as folls:
Row 1: K8, p to end.
Row 2 (dec row): K2 tog, k to end.
Row 3: K8, p to end.
Row 4: Knit to end.
Rows 3 and 4 form the garter st border pattern.
Cont in garter st border pattern, working a dec row (a Row 2)
on rows stated, until 42 (45: 47: 50) sts rem.
Cont straight in st st until work measures 7 (8½: 9½: 10¾) in./18
(22: 24: 27) cm from cast-on edge or desired length, ending
with a purl row.

shape armholes

Bind (cast) off 3 (4: 4: 5) sts at beg of next row. *39 (41: 43: 45) sts*
Work one row straight as before without shaping.

Dec 1 st at armhole edge of foll 4 rows.
Dec 1 st at armhole edge of foll 2 alt rows. *33 (35: 37: 39) sts*
Knit 1 row.
Place these 33 (35: 37: 39) sts on holder.

right front

Using size 6 (4 mm) needles, cast on 48 (52: 54: 58) sts.
Work 1⅛ in./3 cm in garter st (knit every row).
Cont in st st, with a garter st border, dec 1 st at beg of Row
2 and then at non-garter side seam on every foll 6th (6th: 8th:
8th) row as folls:
Row 1: P to last 8 sts, k8.
Row 2 (dec row): K to last 2 sts, k2tog.
Row 3: P to last 8 sts, k8.
Row 4: Knit to end.
Rows 3 and 4 form the garter st border pattern.
Cont in garter st border pattern, working a dec row (a Row 2)
on rows stated, until 42 (45: 47: 50) sts rem.
Cont straight in st st until work measures 7 (8½: 9½: 10¾) in./18
(22: 24: 27) cm from cast-on edge, or desired length, ending
with a knit row.

shape armholes

Bind (cast) off 3 (4: 4: 5) sts at beg of next row. *39 (41: 43: 45) sts*
Work one row straight as before without shaping.
Dec 1 st at armhole edge of foll 4 rows.
Dec 1 st at armhole edge of foll 2 alt rows. *33 (35: 37: 39) sts*
Purl 1 row.
Place these 33 (35: 37: 39) sts on holder.

sleeves (make two alike)

Using size 6 (4 mm) needles, cast on 64 (68: 70: 72) sts.
Work 1⅛ in./3 cm in garter st (knit every row).
Beg with a purl row, cont straight in st st until work measures
7 (7½: 7¾: 8¼) in./18 (19: 20: 21) cm from cast-on edge, ending
with a purl row.

shape sleeve top

Bind (cast) off 3 (4: 4: 5) sts at beg of next 2 rows. *58 (60: 62: 62) sts*

Dec 1 st at each end of foll 4 rows, then at each end of foll 2 alt rows. *46 (48: 50: 50) sts*

Knit 1 row.

Place these 46 (48: 50: 50) sts on holder.

yoke

N.B: when working yoke, due to the decreases, the rib pattern will begin with differing sts in each section every row, so you will have to check sts from the row before to continue your rib pattern; be careful not to end up with seed (moss) st. With WS facing, k8, p25 (27: 29: 31) from left front holder, place marker, p46 (48: 50: 50) from sleeve holder, place marker, p56 (58: 62: 64) from back holder, place marker, p46 (48: 50: 50) from rem sleeve holder, place marker, p25 (27: 29: 31), k8 from right front holder. *214 (224: 236: 242) sts*

Row 1 (RS): K8, *k1, p1, rep from * to 3 sts before marker 1, k3tog, slip marker 1, k1, sl 1, k1, psso, k1, *p1, k1, rep from * to 2 sts before marker 2, k2tog, slip marker 2, k1, sl 1, k1, psso, k1, *p1, k1, rep from * to 2 sts before marker 3, k2tog, slip marker 3, k1, sl 1, k1, psso, k1, *p1, k1, rep from * to 2 sts before marker 4, k2tog, slip marker 4, k1, sl 1, k1, psso, k1, *p1, k1, rep from * to last 8 sts, k8. *205 (215: 227: 233) sts*

Row 2: K8, [work established 1 x 1 rib to 2 sts before marker, p2, slip marker, p1] 4 times, work established 1 x 1 rib to last 8 sts, k8.

Row 3: K8, [work established 1 x 1 rib to 2 sts before marker, k2tog, slip marker, k1, sl 1, k1, psso] 4 times, work established 1 x 1 rib to last 8 sts, k8. *197 (207: 219: 225) sts*

Rep last two rows for yoke pattern until 109 (119: 131: 137) sts rem, ending with a Row 2.

make buttonhole

Row 1: K3, bind (cast) off 3 sts (1 st already on RH needle after bind- [cast-]off), k1, [work 1 x 1 rib to 2 sts before marker, k2tog, slip marker, k1, sl 1, k1, psso] 4 times, work 1 x 1 rib to last 8 sts, k8.

Row 2: K8, [work 1 x 1 rib to 2 sts before marker, p2, slip marker, p1] 4 times, work 1 x 1 rib to garter st border, k2, cast on 3 sts, k3.

Cont in yoke patt as before, dec 8 sts every alt row until 69 (77: 77: 95) sts rem.

Bind (cast) off very loosely in rib.

to finish

Press lightly.

Using mattress stitch, sew each seam and underarm seam in one long seam.

Weave in all ends.

Attach button to garter edging of top left front to correspond with buttonhole.

ribbed cardigan with pockets

This practical cardigan has tiny pockets for anything precious that your little one may want to carry around. Knitting a pocket into the garment is slightly more difficult than sewing on a patch pocket, but it is a great technique to know and gives a sleek, professional finish.

materials

7 (7: 8: 9) x 2 oz/50 g balls of Debbie Bliss Cashmerino DK in shade 09 (cornflower, yarn A), 55% merino wool, 32% microfiber, 12% cashmere, 120 yd/110 m

1 x 2 oz/50 g ball of Debbie Bliss Cashmerino DK in shade 29 (lime, yarn B), 55% merino wool, 32% microfiber, 12% cashmere, 120 yd/110 m

Pair of size 5 (3.75 mm) knitting needles

Pair of size 6 (4 mm) knitting needles

Stitch holders

Tapestry (yarn) needle

8 x ⅝-in./15-mm buttons

Sewing needle and thread

gauge (tension)

20 sts and 32 rows to 4 in./10 cm over 3 x 1 rib stitch on size 6 (4 mm) needles.

Always check gauge (tension) carefully, and adjust needle size if necessary (see page 38).

measurements

TO FIT CHEST SIZE	22¾ in./58 cm	24¾ in./63 cm	26¾ in./68 cm	28¾ in./73 cm
ACTUAL CHEST SIZE	27¾ in./70.5 cm	29½ in./74.5 cm	31 in./78.5 cm	32½ in./82.5 cm
ACTUAL LENGTH	13½ in./34 cm	14¼ in./36 cm	16¼ in./41 cm	17¾ in./45 cm
UNDERARM LENGTH	11 in./28 cm	12¼ in./31 cm	13 in./33 cm	14½ in./37 cm

pockets (make two alike)

Using size 6 (4 mm) needles and yarn A, cast on 15 sts and knit for 3 in./8 cm in st st, leaving all sts on a stitch holder to be knitted into the fronts of cardigan later.

back

Using size 5 (3.75 mm) needles and yarn B, cast on 71 (75: 79: 83) sts.

Work in 1 x 1 rib as folls:

Row 1: K1, *p1, k1 rep from * to end of row.

Row 2: P1, *k1, p1 rep from * to end of row.

Change to yarn A and rep these 2 rows once more.

Cont in yarn A, change to size 6 (4 mm) needles and beg rib stitch patt for main body as folls:

Row 1: K3, *p1, k3 rep from * to end of row.

Row 2: P3, *k1, p3, rep from * to end of row.

These 2 rows form rib patt.

Cont in patt until work measures 7¾ (8¼: 10¼; 11½) in./20 (21: 26: 29) cm from cast-on edge, ending with a WS row.

armhole shaping

Maintaining rib patt, bind (cast) off 4 (5: 5: 5) sts at beg of next 2 rows, then dec 1 st at each end of next 4 rows and following 2 alt rows.

Cont straight on these 51 (53: 57: 61) sts in rib patt until work measures 5 (5½: 5½: 6) in./13 (14: 14: 15) cm from beg of armhole shaping, ending with a WS row.

shoulder shaping

Bind (cast) off 5 sts at beg of next 2 (2: 4: 6) rows.

Bind (cast) off 4 sts at beg of foll 4 (4: 2: 0) rows.

Next row: Bind (cast) off all 25 (27: 29: 31) rem sts.

left front

Using size 5 (3.75 mm) needles and yarn B, cast on 35 (37: 39: 41) sts.

Work in 1 x 1 rib as folls:

Row 1: K1, *p1, k1, rep from * to end of row.

Row 2: P1, *k1, p1 rep from * to end of row.

Change to yarn A and rep these 2 rows once more.

Cont in yarn A, change to size 6 (4 mm) needles and beg rib stitch patt for main body as folls:

Row 1: K2 (0: 2: 0), *p1, k3, rep from * to last 5 sts, p1, k4.

Row 2: P4, *k1, p3, rep from * to last 3 (1: 3: 1) sts, k1, p2 (0: 2: 0).

These 2 rows form rib patt.

Cont in patt until work measures 3½ in./9 cm from cast-on edge, ending with a WS row.

place pocket

Row 1: Work in rib patt across 26 (28: 30: 32) sts, place last 15 sts worked on a st holder, cont in rib patt to end of row.

Next row: Work in rib patt across to sts on the holder. Leave these sts on the holder and cont in rib patt across the 15 sts of one of the pockets knitted previously, ensuring that the right (knit) side of the pocket is facing the wrong side of the front. Work to end of row.

Next row: Work in rib patt across to pocket sts, work pocket sts in rib patt, cont to end of row.

Cont in this way in established rib st, working on the new pocket sts until work is same length as Back to start of armhole shaping, ending with a WS row.

armhole shaping

Next row: Bind (cast) off 4 (5: 5: 5) sts at beg of row, work to end.

Dec 1 st at armhole edge on next 4 rows and foll 2 alt rows. *25 (26: 28: 30) sts*

Work straight until Front is 9 rows shorter than Back to start of shoulder shaping, ending with a RS row.

shape neck

Row 1: Bind (cast) off 7 (8: 9: 10) sts, rib to end of row.

Dec 1 st at neck edge of next 3 rows and 2 foll alt rows. *13 (13: 14: 15) sts*

Row 9 and every foll alt row: Work straight in patt.

Row 10: Bind (cast) off 5 sts, patt to end.

Row 12: Bind (cast) off 4 (4: 5: 5) sts, patt to end.

Work one more row straight.
Bind (cast) off rem 4 (4: 4: 5) sts.

finish pocket

Slip the 15 sts on stitch holder onto a size 5 (3.75 mm) needle. Using yarn A, work 2 rows in 1 x 1 rib, then change to yarn B and work 2 more rows in 1 x 1 rib.

Bind (cast) off all sts.

right front

Using size 5 (3.75 mm) needles and yarn B, cast on 35 (37: 39: 41) sts.

Work in 1 x 1 rib as folls:

Row 1: K1, *p1, k1, rep from * to end of row.

Row 2: P1, *k1, p1 rep from * to end of row.

Change to yarn A and rep these 2 rows once more.

Cont in yarn A, change to size 6 (4 mm) needles and beg rib stitch patt for main body as folls:

Row 1: K4, *p1, k3 rep from * to last 3 (1: 3: 1) sts, p1, k2 (0: 2: 0).

Row 2: P2 (0: 2: 0), *k1, p3, rep from * to last 5 sts, k1, p4.

These 2 rows form rib patt.

Cont in rib patt until work measures 3½ in./9 cm from cast-on edge, ending with a WS row.

place pocket

Row 1: Work in rib patt across 24 sts, place last 15 sts worked on a st holder, cont in rib patt to end of row.

Next row: Work in rib patt across to sts on the holder. Leave these sts on the holder and cont in rib patt across the 15 sts of one of the pockets knitted previously, ensuring that the right (knit) side of the pocket is facing the wrong side of the front. Work to end of row.

Next row: Work in rib patt across to pocket sts, work pocket sts in rib patt, cont to end of row.

Cont in rib st, working on the new pocket sts until work is same length as Back to start of armhole shaping, ending with a RS row.

armhole shaping

Next row: Bind (cast) off 4 (5: 5: 5) sts at beg of row, work to end.

Dec 1 st at armhole edge on next 4 rows and foll 2 alt rows. *25 (26: 28: 30) sts*

Work straight until Front is 8 rows shorter than Back to start of shoulder shaping, ending with a WS row.

shape neck

Row 1: Bind (cast) off 7 (8: 9: 10) sts, rib to end of row.

Dec 1 st at neck edge of next 3 rows and 2 foll alt rows. *13 (13: 14: 15) sts*

Row 9: Work straight in patt.

shoulder shaping

Row 10: Bind (cast) off 5 sts, patt to end.

Row 11: Work straight in patt.

Row 12: Bind (cast) off 4 (4: 5: 5) sts, patt to end.

Work one more row straight.

Bind (cast) off rem 4 (4: 4 :5) sts. Finish pocket as for left front.

sleeves (make two alike)

Using size 5 (3.75 mm) needles and yarn B, cast on 31 (35: 39: 43) sts.

Work in 1 x 1 rib as folls:

Row 1: *K1, p1, rep from * to last st, k1.

Row 2: *P1, k1, rep from * to last st, p1.

Change to yarn A and rep these 2 rows once more.

Cont in yarn A, change to size 6 (4 mm) needles and beg rib stitch patt for main body as folls:

Row 1: *K3, p1, rep from * to last 3 sts, k3.

Row 2: P3, *k1, p3, rep from * to end of row.

These 2 rows form rib patt.

Cont in patt, inc 1 st at each end of next and every foll 5th (6th: 7th: 8th) row until there are 59 (63: 63: 67) sts, fitting increased sts into rib pattern as you knit.

Cont in patt until sleeve measures 11 (12¼: 13: 14½) in./28 (31: 33: 37) cm from cast-on edge, or desired length of sleeve to armhole, ending with a WS row.

shape top of sleeve

Maintaining rib patt, bind (cast) off 4 (5: 5: 5) sts at beg of next 2 rows, then dec 1 st at each end of next 4 rows and following 2 alt rows.

Work one row straight in rib patt.

Bind (cast) off rem 39 (41: 41: 45) sts.

to finish

Block and press all pieces lightly.

Using mattress st, sew shoulder seams.

Fold sleeves in half lengthwise. Matching center top of sleeve to shoulder seam, sew bound-off (cast-off) edge of sleeve to edge of main body.

Sew each side and underarm seam as one long seam.

Weave in all ends.

neck edge

With RS facing and size 5 (3.75 mm) needles, pick up and knit 7 (8: 9: 10) sts from right front neck, 8 sts up side of neck, 25 (27: 29: 31) sts across back neck, 8 sts down left side of neck and 7 (8: 9: 10) sts across left front neck. *55 (59: 63: 67) sts*

Work 4 rows in 1 x 1 rib.

Bind (cast) off all sts loosely in rib.

button band

Using size 6 (4 mm) needles, cast on 6 sts, and work in 1 x 1 rib until work measures 12¼ (13: 15: 16½) in./31 (33: 38: 42) cm.

Bind (cast) off all sts and slipstitch along left front for girls or right front for boys.

buttonhole band

Work a buttonhole band for rem front as folls:

Using size 6 (4 mm) needles, cast on 6 sts.

Work in 1 x 1 rib. On 3rd (3rd: 5th: 5th) row, work buttonhole as folls: K1, p1, k1, yo, k2tog, p1.

Cont in rib patt, working 1 buttonhole row on every foll 13th (14th: 16th: 18th) row until there are 8 buttonholes in total.

Work 4 (3: 4: 4) rows in 1 x 1 rib, bind (cast) off all sts and slipstitch buttonhole band in place along left front (for girls) or right front (for boys).

Sew on eight buttons to correspond with buttonholes.

Sew the pocket lining neatly to the inside of the fronts around the side and bottom edges, using back stitch or mattress stitch.

Weave in all ends.

chunky roll-neck sweater

On a chilly winter's day, an oversized, high-necked sweater is the only thing to wear. This pattern is in very soft yarn, to eliminate scratching around the neck, and has a large, snug pocket to warm the hands.

materials

8 (9: 9: 10) x 2 oz/50 g balls of Debbie Bliss Cashmerino
   Chunky in shade 28 (olive green), 55% merino wool, 33%
   microfiber, 12% cashmere, 71 yd/65 m
Pair of size 9 (5.5 mm) knitting needles
Pair of size 10½ (6.5 mm) knitting needles
Stitch holders
Tapestry (yarn) needle

gauge (tension)

15 sts and 20 rows to 4 in./10 cm over st st on size 10½ (6.5 mm) needles.

Always check gauge (tension) carefully, and adjust needle size if necessary (see page 38).

measurements

TO FIT CHEST SIZE	22¾ in./58 cm	24¾ in./63 cm	26¾ in./68 cm	28¾ in./73 cm
ACTUAL CHEST SIZE	27¼ in./69 cm	29 in./74 cm	31½ in./80 cm	33½ in./ 85 cm
ACTUAL LENGTH	14¼ in./36 cm	15¾ in./40 cm	17¼ in./44 cm	18¾ in./48 cm
UNDERARM LENGTH	11½ in./29 cm	12½ in./32 cm	13½ in./34 cm	14¼ in./36 cm

back

**Using size 9 (5.5 mm) needles, cast on 54 (58: 62: 66) sts.
Work 2 in./5 cm in 2 x 2 rib as folls:
Row 1: K2, *p2, k2, rep from * to end of row.
Row 2: P2, *k2, p2, rep from * to end of row.
Rep last 2 rows for length of rib, ending with a Row 2.
Change to size 10½ (6.5 mm) needles.
Beg with a knit row, work straight in st st until work measures 7¾ (9: 10½: 12) in./20 (23: 27: 30) cm, or desired length to armhole, ending with a purl row.

shape armholes

Working in st st, bind (cast) off 3 sts at beg of next 2 rows, then dec 1 st at each end of every row until 46 (50: 52: 54) sts rem.**
Cont straight in st st without decreasing until Back measures 13½ (15: 16½: 18) in./34 (38: 42: 46) cm, ending with a purl row.

shape shoulders

Working in st st, bind (cast) off 7 (7: 8: 8) sts at beg of next 2 rows, then 6 (7: 7: 7) sts at beg of foll 2 rows. Leave rem 20 (22: 22: 24) sts on holder.

front

Work as for Back between ** and **.
Cont straight in st st without decreasing until Front measures 12 (13½: 15: 16½) in./30 (34: 38: 42) cm, ending with a purl row.

shape left neck

K15 (17: 18: 18), turn and leave rem sts on needle. Cont on these 15 (17: 18: 18) sts for left neck, dec 1 st on neck edge of next and every foll alt row until 13 (14: 15: 15) sts rem.
Work straight on these sts until Front matches Back to start of shoulder shaping, ending with a purl row.

shape left shoulder

Bind (cast) off 7 (7: 8: 8) sts at beg of next row, purl 1 row, then bind (cast) off 6 (7: 7: 7) sts at beg of next row.

shape right neck

With RS facing, slip center 16 (16: 16: 18) neck sts onto a holder, rejoin yarn to rem 15 (17: 18: 18) sts of right neck, dec 1 st at neck edge of every foll alt row until 13 (14: 15: 15) sts rem.
Work straight on these sts until Front matches Back to start of shoulder shaping, ending with a knit row.

shape right shoulder

Bind (cast) off 7 (7: 8: 8) sts at beg of next row, purl 1 row, then bind (cast) off 6 (7: 7: 7) sts at beg of next row.

sleeves (make two alike)

Using size 9 (5.5 mm) needles, cast on 22 (26: 30: 34) sts.
Work in 2 x 2 rib as folls:
Row 1: K2, *p2, k2, rep from * to end of row.
Row 2: P2, *k2, p2, rep from * to end of row.
Rep last 2 rows until rib measures 2 in./5 cm, ending with a Row 2.
Change to size 10½ (6.5 mm) needles.
Beg with a knit row, work in st st, inc 1 st at each end of 3rd and every foll 3rd (3rd: 4th: 6th) row until there are 42 (46: 48: 52) sts.
Work straight in st st until work measures 11½ (12½: 13¼: 14) in./29 (32: 34: 36) cm, or desired sleeve length to underarm, ending with a purl row.

shape sleeve top

Bind (cast) off 3 sts at beg of next 2 rows, then dec 1 st at each end of every row until 34 (38: 36: 38) sts rem.
Dec 1 st at each end of every alt row until 28 (32: 32: 36) sts rem. Bind (cast) off all sts.

pocket

Using size 10½ (6.5 mm) needles, cast on 22 sts.
Work in 2 x 2 rib as folls:
Row 1: K2, *p2, k2, rep from * to end.

Bind (cast) off in rib.

to finish
Block and press all pieces.
Using mattress stitch, sew left shoulder seam.

neck edging
With RS facing and using size 9 (5.5 mm) needles, join yarn to back neck.
Knit across 20 (22: 22: 24) sts, pick up and knit 11 (12: 12: 12) sts down left side of neck, knit across 16 (16: 16: 18) sts at center front neck, then pick up and knit 11 (12: 12: 12) sts up right side of neck. *58 (62: 62: 66) sts*
Work on these sts in 2 x 2 rib for 3½ (3½: 4: 4) in./9 (9: 10: 10) cm as folls:
Row 1: K2, *p2, k2, rep from * to end.
Row 2: P2, *k2, p2, rep from * to end.
Rep these two rows for length of rib.
Bind (cast) off all sts in rib.

seams, sleeves, and pockets
Using mattress stitch, sew rem shoulder seam, reversing for the roll neck.
Fold sleeves in half lengthwise.
Matching center top of sleeve to shoulder seam, sew bound-off (cast-off) edge of sleeve to edge of main sweater body.
Sew side seam and underarm seams in one long seam on each side.
Center the pocket on the front of the sweater, immediately above the rib at the base of the sweater, and stitch along the two st st edges, leaving the ribbed sides free.
Weave in all the loose ends of yarn.

Row 2: P2, *k2, p2, rep from * to end.
Rep these two rows until rib measures 1¼ in./3 cm, ending with a Row 2.
Beg with a knit row, work straight in st st for 4¼ (4¾: 4¾: 5¼) in./11 (12: 12: 13) cm from end of rib.
Work 1¼ in./3 cm straight in 2 x 2 rib.

cable v-neck top

This top works well in a contemporary wardrobe, as the neutral colorway goes well with all kinds of outfits. The cables are very simple, and the fisherman- (aran-) weight yarn gives great stitch definition. Cables show up best in lighter shades; there's no point in spending a lot of time knitting a beautiful texture only for it not to show up in a dark yarn.

materials

3 (4: 4: 5) x 2 oz/ 50 g balls of Mission Falls 1824 wool in
  001 (natural, yarn A), 100% merino superwash wool, 85 yd/78 m
1 x 2 oz/ 50 g ball of Mission falls 1824 wool in shade 021
  (denim, yarn B), 100% merino superwash wool, 85 yd/78 m
Pair of size 8 (5 mm) knitting needles
Pair of size 7 (4.5 mm) knitting needles
Cable needle and stitch holder
Tapestry (yarn) needle

gauge (tension)

18 sts and 24 rows to 4 in./10 cm over st st on size 8 (5 mm) needles. Always check gauge (tension) carefully, and adjust needle size if necessary (see page 38).

special abbreviations

C4B = Cable 4 back. Place next 2 sts on a cable needle and hold at back of work, k next 2 sts, then knit 2 sts from cable needle.

C4F = Cable 4 front. Place next 2 sts on a cable needle and hold at front of work, k next 2 sts, then knit 2 sts from cable needle.

C6B = Cable 6 back. Place next 3 sts on a cable needle and hold at back of work, k next 3 sts, then knit 3 sts from cable needle.

C6F = Cable 6 front. Place next 3 sts on a cable needle and hold at front of work, k next 3 sts, then knit 3 sts from cable needle.

measurements

TO FIT CHEST SIZE	20 in./51 cm	22 in./56 cm	24 in./61 cm	26 in./66 cm
ACTUAL CHEST SIZE	21¼ in./54 cm	23½ in./60 cm	25½ in./65 cm	27¼ in./69 cm
ACTUAL LENGTH	12 in./30 cm	13½ in./34 cm	15 in./38 cm	16½ in./42 cm

Rep these two rows once more.

Row 5: K5 (8: 10: 12), p2, C6B, p2, k8, p2, C4B, C4F, p2, k8, p2, C6F, p2, k5 (8: 10: 12).

Row 6 (and every other row): P5 (8: 10: 12), k2, p6, k2, [p8, k2] three times, p6, k2, p5 (8: 10: 12).

Row 7: K5 (8: 10: 12), p2, k6, p2, [k8, p2] three times, k6, p2, k5 (8: 10: 12).

Row 9: Rep Row 7.

Row 11: K5 (8: 10: 12), p2, k6, p2, k8, p2, C4B, C4F, p2, k8, p2, k6, p2, k5 (8: 10: 12).

Row 13: Rep Row 7.

Row 15: Rep Row 7.

Row 17: K5 (8: 10: 12), p2, C6B, p2, k8, p2, C4B, C4F, p2, k8, p2, C6F, p2, k5 (8: 10: 12).

Rows 6–17 form pattern.

Cont in pattern until work measures 6¼ (7½: 8½: 9¾) in./16 (19: 22: 25) cm, ending with a WS row. **

shape armholes

Maintaining continuity of rib pattern, bind (cast) off 5 (6: 7: 7) sts at beg of next 2 rows, then dec 1 st at each end of next 3 rows and foll 4 (4: 5: 5) alt rows. *34 (38: 38: 42) sts*

Cont in rib pattern until work measures 11½ (13: 14½: 16) in./ 29 (33: 37: 41) cm, ending with a WS row.

shape back neck and shoulders

Maintaining continuity of rib pattern, patt across 9 (10: 10: 11) sts, turn and leave rem sts on holder. Working on these 9 (10: 10: 11) sts in patt for right side of neck, dec 1 st at neck edge of next and foll alt rows.

Next row: Bind (cast) off 4 (4: 4: 5) sts, patt to end.

Next row: Bind (cast) off rem 3 (4: 4: 4) sts.

Leaving center 16 (18: 18: 20) sts on holder, join yarn to 9 (10: 10: 11) sts for left neck.

Reverse shaping to match opposite side.

front

Work as Back from ** to **, then shape armholes as follows:

back

**Using size 7 (4.5 mm) needles and yarn A, cast on 58 (64: 68: 72) sts. Work 10 rows in 1 x 1 rib.

Change to size 8 (5 mm) needles and begin pattern as folls:

Row 1: K5 (8: 10: 12), p2, k6, p2, [k8, p2] three times, k6, p2, k5 (8: 10: 12).

Row 2: P5 (8: 10: 12), k2, p6, k2, [p8, k2] three times, p6, k2, p5 (8: 10: 12).

Maintaining continuity of rib pattern, bind (cast) off 5 (6: 7: 7) sts at beg of next 2 rows, then divide for neck as folls:

divide for neck

Dec 1 st at beg of row, patt until 23 (25: 26: 28) sts on needle, turn work, leaving rem 24 (26: 27: 29) sts on holder for right side of neck. Dec 1 st at each end of next row and cont in patt, decreasing 1 st at armhole edge of foll row and next 4 (4: 5: 5) alt rows while at the same time dec 1 st every 3rd row at neck edge. After armhole decreases have been made, cont working the neck decreases every 3rd row until 7 (8: 8: 9) sts rem, then work straight until work measures the same length as Back to shoulder shaping, ending with a WS row.

shape shoulders

Bind (cast) off 4 (4: 4: 5) sts, patt to end of row.
Next row: Patt across.
Next row: Bind (cast) off rem sts.
Rejoin yarn to right side of neck at neck edge, with right side of work facing, patt across row, dec 1 st at end of row.
Dec 1 st at each end of next row and cont in patt, decreasing 1 st at armhole edge of foll row and next 4 (4: 5: 5) alt rows while at the same time dec 1 st every 3rd row at neck edge. After armhole decreases have been made, cont working the neck decreases every 3rd row until 7 (8: 8: 9) sts rem, then work straight until work measures the same length as Back to shoulder shaping, ending with a RS row.

shape shoulders

Bind (cast) off 4 (4: 4: 5) sts, patt to end of row.
Next row: Patt across.
Next row: Bind (cast) off rem sts.

edgings

Join together right shoulders using mattress stitch and yarn A. Using yarn A, join yarn to top of left neck edge, with RS facing. Using size 7 (4.5 mm) needles, pick up and knit 28 (30: 34: 38) sts down front left neck edge, 1 st from center of v, 28 (30: 34: 38) sts up front right neck, 4 sts down back right neck, 16 (18: 18: 20) sts from holder at back neck and 4 sts up back left neck. *81 (87: 95: 105) sts*

Row 1: [K1, p1] 26 (28: 30: 33) times, p center st, [p1, k1] to end of row.
Row 2: Change to yarn B and rib to 2 sts before center v st, k2tog, k center st, sl 1, k1, psso, rib to end of row.
Row 3: Rib to 1 st before center v st, p3, rib to end of row.
Row 4: Change to yarn A and work 1 more rib row as Row 2. Bind (cast) off all sts in rib.
Using mattress stitch, join left shoulder seam and ribbed edge seam.
Join yarn A to bottom of armhole, with RS facing. Using size 7 (4.5 mm) needles, pick up and knit 62 (66: 70: 74) sts along armhole opening, turn and work 4 rows in 1 x 1 rib. Bind (cast) off all sts in rib.
Join yarn A to rem armhole and complete to match other edge.
Sew up side seams in mattress st.
Press lightly and weave in all ends.

smock top

Knitwear is not just for winter; there are many yarns made from breathable, summery fibers, which are soft and easy to wear. Combined with the durability of cotton, soy (soya) is a great choice for this cool smock. Most of the top is knitted in plain old stockinette (stocking) stitch, but it has a decorative picot hem and an optional heart-shaped embellishment.

materials

4 (4: 5: 5: 5) x 2 oz/50 g balls of Sublime Soya Cotton in shade 88 (pomegranate), 50% soya, 50% cotton, 120 yd/110 m

1 x 2 oz/50g ball of Sublime Soya Cotton in shade 84 (comfrey), 50% soya, 50% cotton, 120 yd/110 m (or small amounts of contrasting yarn) for embellishment

Pair of size 6 (4 mm) knitting needles

Stitch holders

Tapestry (yarn) needle

8 x ⅜-in./10-mm buttons

Sewing needle and thread

gauge (tension)

20 sts and 27 rows to 4 in./10 cm over st st on size 6 (4 mm) knitting needles.

Always check gauge (tension) carefully, and adjust needle size if necessary (see page 38).

measurements

TO FIT APPROX. CHEST SIZE	22 in./56 cm	23½ in./60 cm	25 in./64 cm	26¾ in./68 cm	28¼ in./72 cm
ACTUAL CHEST SIZE	23½ in./60 cm	25 in./64 cm	26¾ in./68 cm	28¾ in./72 cm	30 in./76 cm
ACTUAL LENGTH	12¼ in./31 cm	13½ in./34 cm	15½ in./39 cm	15¾ in./40 cm	17 in./43 cm

picot hem

Using size 6 (4 mm) needles and main yarn, cast on 145 (153: 165: 173: 181) sts.

Beg with a knit row, work 4 rows in st st.

Work one row eyelet holes for picot hem, as folls:

K1, *yo, k2tog, rep from * to end of row.

Beg with a purl row, work 3 rows in st st.

main body

Cont main body as folls:

Row 1: Knit to end.

Row 2: K5, p to last 5 sts, k5.

Rep these two rows for length of body, making 1 buttonhole in garter st border at beg of row on 3rd (1st: 7th: 3rd: 9th) and foll 10th (12th: 12th: 14th: 14th) rows throughout as folls:

K2, yo, k2tog, k1, k to end of row.

At the same time dec on next and every foll 6th (8th: 8th: 8th: 10th) row as folls:

Next row: K17 (18: 20: 21: 22), k2tog, k34 (36: 39: 41: 43), sl 1, k1, psso, k35 (37: 39: 41: 43), k2tog, k34 (36: 39: 41: 43), sl 1, k1, psso, k17 (18: 20: 21: 22). *141 (149: 161: 169: 177) sts*

Work in this way until 125 (133: 141: 149: 157) sts rem.

Cont straight in st st without decreasing until work measures 6¼ (7: 8¼: 9: 10¼) in./16 (18: 21: 23: 26) cm from eyelet holes row, ending with a WS row.

shape armholes and divide for front and back
left back

K32 (34: 36: 38: 40), turn, leaving rem 93 (99: 105: 111: 117) sts on holder, work on these 32 (34: 36: 38: 40) sts for left back as folls:

Row 1: Bind (cast) off 3 (3: 3: 4: 4) sts, p to last 5 sts, k5. *29 (31: 33: 34: 36) sts*

Dec 1 st at armhole edge of next 3 (3: 3: 4: 4) rows. *26 (28: 30: 30: 32) sts*

Work straight in patt, remembering to cont making buttonholes on every 10th (12th: 12th: 14th: 14th) row, until work measures 5 (5½: 5½: 6: 6) in./13 (14: 14: 15: 15) cm from start of armhole shaping, ending with a RS row.

Bind (cast) off 4 sts at beg of next row.

Then bind (cast) off 4 (4: 5: 5: 5) sts at beg of foll 2 alt rows.

Leave rem 14 (15: 16: 16: 18) sts on holder for back left neck.

front

With RS facing, rejoin yarn to 93 (99: 105: 111: 117) unworked sts.

Bind (cast) off 3 (3: 3: 4: 4) sts, (1 st left on RH needle), k57 (61: 65: 68: 72), turn, leaving rem 32 (34: 36: 38: 40) sts on holder for right back.

Cont to work on 58 (62: 66: 69: 73) sts for front.

Bind (cast) off 3 (3: 3: 4: 4) sts, p to end of row. *55 (59: 63: 65: 68) sts*

Dec 1 st at each end of next 3 (3: 3: 4: 4) rows. *49 (53: 57: 57: 61) sts*

Cont straight until work measures 3 (3½: 3½: 4: 4) in./8 (9: 9: 10: 10) cm from start of armhole shaping, ending with a purl row.

divide for neck

K19 (19: 21: 21: 22), bind (cast) off 11 (15: 15: 15: 17) sts, k to end of row.

Cont on these 19 (19: 21: 21: 22) sts for right neck as folls:

Dec 1 st at neck edge on foll 5 (4: 5: 5: 6) rows, then dec 1 st at neck edge on 2 foll alt rows. *12 (13: 14: 14: 14) sts*

Work straight on these sts until work measures 5 (5½: 5½: 6: 6) in./13 (14: 14: 15: 15) cm from start of armhole shaping, ending with a knit row.

shape right shoulder

Bind (cast) off 4 sts at beg of next row.

Then bind (cast) off 4 (4: 5: 5: 5) sts at beg of foll 2 alt rows.

shape left neck

With WS facing, rejoin yarn to left side of neck.

Dec 1 st at neck edge on foll 5 (4: 5: 5: 6) rows, then dec 1 st at neck edge on 2 foll alt rows. *12 (13: 14: 14: 14) sts*

Work straight on these sts until work measures 5 (5½: 5½: 6: 6) in./13 (14: 14: 15: 15) cm from start of armhole shaping, ending with a purl row.

shape left shoulder

Bind (cast) off 4 sts at beg of next row.

Then bind (cast) off 4 (4: 5: 5: 5) sts at beg of foll 2 alt rows.

right back

With RS facing, rejoin yarn to rem 32 (34: 36: 38: 40) sts on holder, bind (cast) off 3 (3: 3: 4: 4) sts, k to end of row. *29 (31: 33: 34: 36) sts*

Dec 1 st at armhole edge of next 3 (3: 3: 4: 4) rows. *26 (28: 30: 30: 32) sts*

Cont straight until work measures 5 (5½: 5½: 6: 6) in./13 (14: 14: 15: 15) cm from start of armhole shaping, ending with a WS row.

Bind (cast) off 4 sts at beg of next row.

Then bind (cast) off 4 (4: 5: 5: 5) sts at beg of foll alt row.

Work 1 row.

Bind (cast) off 4 (5: 5: 5: 5) sts at beg of next row, cut yarn and leave rem 14 (15: 16: 16: 18) sts unworked on holder for back right neck.

to finish

Turn up picot hem and sew neatly onto ws of work so that scalloped edge shows. Block and press hem and top.

armhole edgings

With RS facing, attach yarn to shoulder of one armhole. Using size 6 (4 mm) needles and main yarn, pick up and knit 65 (70: 70: 75: 75) sts evenly all around armhole. Turn and work 1 row knit on these sts.

Bind (cast) off all sts loosely.

Sew up shoulder seam.

Complete other armhole in the same way.

neck edging

With RS facing, attach yarn to left back neck. Using size 6 (4 mm) needles, knit across 14 (15: 16: 16: 18) sts on left neck holder, pick up and knit 18 sts down left front neck, pick up and knit 13 (14: 14: 14: 16) sts from center front, 18 sts up right neck and knit across 14 (15: 16: 16: 18) sts from right back

holder. *77 (80: 82: 82: 88) sts*

Turn and work 1 row knit on these sts.

Bind (cast) off all sts loosely.

Weave in ends.

optional heart-shaped embellishment

Using size 6 (4 mm) needles and main yarn, cast on 3 sts.

Row 1: K1, p1, k1.

Row 2: Inc 1, p1, inc 1.

Row 3: P1, k1, p1, k1, p1.

Row 4: Inc 1, k1, p1, k1, inc 1. *7 sts*

Row 5: K1, p1, k1, p1, k1, p1, k1.

Row 6: Inc 1, p1, *k1, p1, rep from * to last st, inc 1. *9 sts*

Row 7: P1, *k1, p1, rep from * to end of row.

Row 8: Inc 1, k1, *p1, k1, rep from * to last st, inc 1. *11 sts*

Row 9: K1, *p1, k1, rep from * to end of row.

Row 10: Inc 1, p1, *k1, p1, from * to last st, inc 1. *13 sts*

Row 11: P1, *k1, p1, rep from * to end of row.

Row 12: Inc 1, k1, *p1, k1, rep from * to last st, inc 1. *15 sts*

Rows 13–15: K1, *p1, k1, rep from * to end of row.

Row 16: K2tog, k1, p1, k1, p1, k2tog, turn, leaving rem sts unworked.

Row 17: [K1, p1] three times.

Row 18: K2tog, p1, k1, k2tog. *4 sts*

Row 19: [P1, k1] twice.

Row 20: [K2tog] twice.

Bind (cast) off rem sts.

Rejoin yarn to inner edge of rem sts.

K2tog, k1, p1, k1, k2tog. *5 sts*

*P1, k1, rep from * to last st, p1.

K2tog, p1, k2tog. *3 sts*

Sl 1, k2tog, psso.

Fasten off last st.

Attach heart motif with contrasting yarn or any yarn of your choice to bottom front of top.

Sew on buttons to right back garter st border, to correspond with buttonholes on opposite side.

sweater with shoulder buttons

This sweater is born out of nostalgia for vintage children's clothes. The tiny cables and buttoned yoke are beautifully delicate, and the warm peach shade allows the cables to be shown in all their glory.

materials

4 (4: 5: 6: 7) x 2 oz/50 g balls of Rowan Pure Wool 4-ply in
  shade 444, 100% wool, 174 yd/160 m
Pair of size 2 (3 mm) knitting needles
Pair of size 3 (3.25 mm) knitting needles
Cable needle
6 x ⅜-in./10-mm buttons
Tapestry (yarn) needle

gauge (tension)

28 sts and 36 rows to 4 in./10 cm over st st on size 3 (3.25 mm) needles. Always check gauge (tension) carefully, and adjust needle size if necessary (see page 38).

special abbreviations

C4R = Cable 4 right. Place next 3 sts on a cable needle and hold at the back of work, k next st, then knit 3 sts from cable needle.
C4B = Cable 4 back. Place next 2 sts on a cable needle and hold at back of work, k next 2 sts, then knit 2 sts from cable needle.

measurements

ACTUAL CHEST SIZE	24 in./61 cm	25½ in./65 cm	27½ in./70 cm	29 in./74 cm	30¾ in./78 cm
ACTUAL LENGTH	12½ in./32 cm	13¾ in./35 cm	15 in./38 cm	15¾ in./40 cm	16½ in./42 cm
UNDERARM SLEEVE LENGTH	10½ in./27 cm	11½ in./29 cm	12½ in./32 cm	13¼ in./34 cm	14 in./36 cm

back

**Using size 2 (3 mm) needles, cast on 86 (92: 98: 104: 110) sts and work in rib pattern as folls:

Row 1: K3, *p2, k4, rep from * to last 5 sts, p2, k3.

Row 2: P3, *k2, p4, rep from * to last 5 sts, k2, p3.

Row 3: K3, *p2, k4, rep from * to last 5 sts, p2, k3.

Rows 2 and 3 form rib pattern.

Row 4: Rep Row 2.

Row 5 (cable row): K3, *p2, C4R, rep from * to last 5 sts, p2, k3.

Rows 6–10: Work 5 rows in rib pattern beg with Row 2.

Row 11: Rep Row 5 (cable row).

Rows 12–14: Work 3 rows in rib pattern beg with Row 2.

Change to size 3 (3.25 mm) needles. Cont in st st, beg with a knit row. ** Work until Back measures 7 (7¾: 9: 9½: 9¾) in./18 (20: 23: 24: 25) cm from cast-on, ending with a purl row. (Knit more or fewer rows to fit your child's height.)

shape armholes

Bind (cast) off 5 (5: 7: 7: 8) sts at beg of next 2 rows, then dec 1 st at each end of foll 4 (4: 5: 5: 5) rows. Purl 0 (0: 1: 1: 1) row. *68 (74: 74: 80: 84) sts*

shape raglan neckline

Row 1: K1, sl 1, k1, psso, k to last 3 sts, k2tog, k1.

Next row: Purl to end.

Rep these 2 rows until 24 (26: 26: 28: 30) sts rem, ending with a purl row, then bind (cast) off all sts.

front

Work as Back between ** and **.

Work until Front measures 6 (6¾: 7¾: 8¼: 8½) in./15 (17: 20: 21: 22) cm from cast-on, ending with purl row. Beg rib patt as folls:

Row 1 (RS): *P2, k4, rep from * to last 2 sts, p2.

Row 2: *K2, p4, rep from * to last 2 sts, k2.

Rows 3–4: Rep Rows 1 and 2.

Row 5 (cable row): *P2, C4B, rep from * to last 2 sts, p2.

Row 6: *K2, p4, rep from * to last 2 sts, k2.

Row 7: *P2, k4, rep from * to last 2 sts, p2.

Rows 8–12: Rep Rows 6 and 7 twice more, then rep Row 6 again.

Row 13: Rep Row 5 (cable row).

Rows 6–13 form cabled rib pattern.

Cont in cabled rib pattern until Front measures the same as Back up to armhole shaping, ending with a WS row.

shape armholes

Bind (cast) off 5 (5: 7: 7: 8) sts at beg of next 2 rows, then dec 1 st at each end of foll 4 (4: 5: 5: 5) rows. Purl 0 (0: 1: 1: 1) row. *68 (74: 74: 80: 84) sts*

shape raglan neckline

Row 1: K1, sl 1, k1, psso, work cabled rib patt to last 3 sts, k2tog, k1.

Next row: P2, rib patt to last 2 sts, p2.

Maintaining cabled rib pattern, rep last 2 rows until 28 (30: 30: 32: 34) sts rem, ending with a WS row, then bind (cast) off all sts.

sleeves (make 2)

Using size 2 (3 mm) needles, cast on 38 (44: 50: 56: 58) sts and work in rib pattern as folls:

Row 1: K3 (3: 3: 3: 4), *p2, k4, rep from * to last 5 (5: 5: 5: 6) sts, p2, k3 (3: 3: 3: 4).

Row 2: P3 (3: 3: 3: 4), *k2, p4, rep from * to last 5 (5: 5: 5: 6) sts, k2, p3 (3: 3: 3: 4).

Row 3: K3 (3: 3: 3: 4), *p2, k4, rep from * to last 5 (5: 5: 5: 6) sts, p2, k3 (3: 3: 3: 4).

Rows 2 and 3 form rib pattern.

Row 4: Rep Row 2.

Row 5 (cable row): K3 (3: 3: 3: 4), *p2, C4R, rep from * to last 5 (5: 5: 5: 6) sts, p2, k3 (3: 3: 3: 4).

Rows 6–10: Work 5 rows in rib pattern beg with Row 2.

Row 11: Rep Row 5 (cable row).

Rows 12–14: Work 3 rows in rib pattern beg with Row 2.

Change to size 3 (3.25 mm) needles. Cont in st st, beg with a knit row.

Inc 1 st at each end of row on 5th and every foll 4th (5th: 6th: 6th: 6th) row until 66 (72: 78: 84: 90) sts rem, then work straight until sleeve measures 9½ (10¼: 11½: 12¼: 13) in./24 (26: 29: 31: 33) cm from cast-on, or until 1¼ in./3 cm less than desired underarm length, ending with a purl row.

Beg cabled rib pattern as folls:

Row 1: K2, *p2, k4, rep from * to last 4 sts, p2, k2.

Row 2: P2, *k2, p4, rep from * to last 4 sts, k2, p2.

Rows 3–4: Rep Rows 1 and 2.

Row 5 (cable row): K2, *p2, C4B, rep from * to last 4 sts, p2, k2.

Row 6: P2, *k2, p4, rep from * to last 4 sts, k2, p2.

Row 7: K2, *p2, k4, rep from * to last 4 sts, p2, k2.

Rows 8–12: Rep Rows 6 and 7 twice more, then rep Row 6 again.

Row 13: Rep Row 5 (cable row).

Rows 6–13 form cabled rib pattern.

Cont in patt until sleeve measures 10½ (11½: 12½: 13¼: 14) in./ 27 (29: 32: 34: 36) cm from cast-on, ending with a WS row.

shape top of sleeve

Bind (cast) off 5 (5: 7: 7: 8) sts at beg of next 2 rows, then dec 1 st at each end of foll 4 (4: 5: 5: 5) rows. Purl 0 (0: 1: 1: 1) row. *48 (54: 54: 60: 64) sts*

shape raglan neckline

Row 1: K1, sl 1, k1, psso, work cabled rib patt to last 3 sts, k2tog, k1.

Next row: P2, rib patt to last 2 sts, p2.

Maintaining cabled rib pattern, rep last 2 rows until 8 (10: 10: 12: 14) sts rem, ending with a RS row.

right sleeve only

Next row: Patt to end of row.

Next row: Bind (cast) off 2 (3: 3: 4: 5) sts, patt to last 3 sts, k2tog, k1.

Rep these 2 rows once more.

Patt across row, then bind (cast) off rem 2 sts.

left sleeve only

Next row: Bind (cast) off 2 (3: 3: 4: 5) sts, patt to end of row.

Next row: K1, sl 1, k1, psso, patt to end of row.

Rep these 2 rows once more.

Patt across row, then bind (cast) off rem 2 sts.

to finish

Join Sleeves to Back along raglan edges using mattress stitch. With RS facing, using size 2 (3 mm) needles, attach yarn to top of right sleeve. Pick up and knit 16 (18: 18: 20: 22) sts from top of right sleeve, 26 (26: 26: 30: 30) sts from back, and 16 (18: 18: 20: 22) sts from top of left sleeve. *58 (62: 62: 70: 74) sts*

Turn and work in 2 x 2 rib as folls:

P2, *k2, p2, rep from * to end of row.

Work 3 more rows in 2 x 2 rib, then bind (cast) off all sts in rib.

Using mattress stitch, sew Front and Back together along side seams, and join sleeves along underarm.

Sew front armhole shaping seams to corresponding sleeve armhole shapings, leaving raglan shaping free.

With RS facing, using size 2 (3 mm) needles, attach yarn to start of raglan shaping at bottom of left front neck. Pick up and knit 36 (40: 40: 44: 48) sts to neck. Turn and work in 2 x 2 rib as folls:

*P2, k2, rep from * to end of row.

Work one more row in rib.

Buttonhole row: Rib 10 (12: 12: 14: 16) sts, yo, k2tog, rib across next 14 (16: 16: 16: 18) sts, yo, k2tog, rib to end of row.

Work one more row in rib, then bind (cast) off all sts in rib.

With RS facing, using size 2 (3 mm) needles, attach yarn to top of raglan shaping at right front neck. Pick up and knit 36 (40: 40: 44: 48) sts along raglan shaping. Turn and work in 2 x 2 rib as folls:

*K2, p2, rep from * to end of row. Work one more row in rib.

Buttonhole row: Rib 8 (8: 8: 10: 10) sts, yo, k2tog, rib across next 14 (16: 16: 16: 18) sts, yo, k2tog, rib to end of row.

Work one more row rib, then bind (cast) off all sts in rib.

With RS facing and using size 2 (3 mm) needles, attach yarn to right neck, pick up and knit 4 sts along ribbing, then 26 (30: 30: 34: 34) sts along cables, then 4 sts along ribbing on other end. *34 (38: 38: 42: 42) sts*

Turn and work in 2 x 2 rib as folls:

P2, *k2, p2, rep from * to end of row.

Buttonhole row: K2, p2, yo, k2tog, rib to last 6 sts, k2tog, yo, p2, k2.

Work 2 more rows in rib, then bind (cast) off all sts in rib.

Attach buttons to back neck ribbing and raglan edging to correspond with buttonholes.

Press lightly and weave in all ends.

hooded cardigan

One way to instantly update a cardigan is to add a hood.
Whether worn up or down, it looks modern and cute and can
be worn by both boys and girls. It is also easier to knit than it
looks; if you can knit a collar, you can also knit a hood.

materials

7 (8: 8: 9) x 2 oz/50 g balls of RYC Cashsoft DK in shade 521
  (opulence), 57% extra fine merino, 33% microfiber, 10%
  cashmere, 142 yd/130 m
Pair of size 4 (3.5 mm) knitting needles
Pair of size 6 (4 mm) knitting needles
Stitch holders

8 x ⅝-in./15-mm buttons
Tapestry (yarn) needle

gauge (tension)

22 sts and 28 rows to 4 in./10 cm over st st on size 6 (4 mm)
needles. Always check gauge (tension) carefully, and adjust
needle size if necessary (see page 38).

measurements

APPROX. CHEST SIZE	23½ in./60 cm	25 in./64 cm	26¾ in./68 cm	28¼ in./72 cm
ACTUAL CHEST SIZE	26¾ in./68 cm	28¼ in./72 cm	30 in./76 cm	31 in./79 cm
ACTUAL BACK LENGTH	13¾ in./35 cm	15 in./38 cm	16¼ in./41 cm	17½ in./44 cm
UNDERARM LENGTH	12 in./30 cm	12½ in./32 cm	13½ in./34 cm	14¼ in./36 cm

clothes

back

Using size 4 (3.5 mm) needles, cast on 77 (81: 85: 89) sts.
Work in 1 x 1 rib as folls:
Row 1: K1, * p1, k1, rep from * to end of row.
Row 2: P1, * k1, p1, rep from * to end of row.
Rep last 2 rows for ¾ in./2 cm, ending with a Row 2.
Change to size 6 (4 mm) needles and cont in st st, beg with a
knit row. Cont in st st until work measures 7¾ (8¾: 9¾: 10½)
in./20 (22: 25: 27) cm, ending with a purl row.

shape armholes

Bind (cast) off 4 (4: 5: 5) sts at beg of next 2 rows, then dec 1 st
at each end of next 3 rows, then 3 foll alt rows. *57 (61: 63: 67) sts*
Cont straight in st st until work measures 5 (5½: 5½: 6) in./13 (14:
14: 15) cm from beg of armhole shaping, ending with a purl row.

shape shoulders

Bind (cast) off 4 sts at beg of next 4 rows, then bind (cast) off
4 (5: 5: 6) sts at beg of next 2 rows. Leave rem sts on a holder.
33 (35: 37: 39) sts

left front

Using size 4 (3.5 mm) needles, cast on 37 (39: 41: 43) sts.
Work in 1 x 1 rib as folls:
Row 1: K1, *p1, k1, rep from * to end of row.
Row 2: P1, *k1, p1, rep from * to end of row.
Rep last 2 rows for ¾ in./2 cm, ending with a Row 2.
Change to size 6 (4 mm) needles.
Beg with a knit row, cont in st st until work measures same as
Back to start of armhole shaping, ending with a purl row.

shape armhole

Bind (cast) off 4 (4: 5: 5) sts at beg of next row, then dec 1 st at
armhole edge of next 3 rows, then dec 1 st at armhole edge of
3 foll alt rows. *27 (29: 30: 32) sts*
Work straight on these sts until Front is 11 rows shorter than
Back to start of shoulder shaping, ending with a knit row.

shape neck

Bind (cast) off 9 (10: 11: 12) sts, p to end of row.

Dec 1 st at neck edge of next 3 rows, then dec 1 st at neck
edge of 3 foll alt rows.
Work one row.

shape shoulder

Bind (cast) off 4 sts at beg of next and foll alt row, then bind
(cast) off 4 (5: 5: 6) sts at beg of foll alt row.

right front

Using size 4 (3.5 mm) needles, cast on 37 (39: 41: 43) sts.
Work in 1 x 1 rib as folls:
Row 1: K1, *p1, k1, rep from * to end of row.
Row 2: P1, *k1, p1, rep from * to end of row.
Rep last 2 rows for ¾ in./2 cm, ending with a Row 2.
Change to size 6 (4 mm) needles.
Beg with a knit row, cont in st st until work measures same as
Back to start of armhole shaping, ending with a knit row.

shape armhole

Bind (cast) off 4 (4: 5: 5) sts at beg of next row, then dec 1 st at
armhole edge of next 3 rows, then at armhole edge of foll 3 alt
rows. *27 (29: 30: 32) sts*
Work straight on these sts until Front is 10 rows shorter than
Back to start of shoulder shaping, ending with a purl row.

shape neck

Bind (cast) off 9 (10: 11: 12) sts, k to end of row.
Dec 1 st at neck edge of next 3 rows, then 3 foll alt rows.
Work one row.

shape shoulder

Bind (cast) off 4 sts at beg of next and foll alt row, then bind
(cast) off 4 (5: 5: 6) sts at beg of foll alt row.

sleeves (make two alike)

Using size 4 (3.5 mm) needles, cast on 37 (41: 45: 49) sts.
Work in 1 x 1 rib as folls:
Row 1: K1, *p1, k1, rep from * to end of row.
Row 2: P1, *k1, p1, rep from * to end of row.
Rep last 2 rows for ¾ in./2 cm, ending with a Row 2.

Change to size 6 (4 mm) needles.

Beg with a knit row, cont in st st, inc 1 st at each end of row on 3rd and every foll 4th (6th: 6th: 6th) row until there are 63 (67: 69: 73) sts.

Work straight in st st without inc until sleeve measures 12 (12¾: 13½: 14¼) in./30 (32: 34: 36) cm or desired length, ending with a purl row.

shape sleeve top

Bind (cast) off 4 sts at beg of next 4 rows, then bind (cast) off 4 (5: 5: 6) sts at beg of next 2 rows. 39 (41: 43: 45) sts
Knit one row.
Bind (cast) off all sts.

joining seams

Using mattress stitch, sew shoulder seams, attach sleeves to armholes, and sew side seam and underarm seam continuously at both sides.

hood

Join yarn to right front neck. Using size 6 (4 mm) needles and with RS facing, pick up and knit 9 (10: 11: 12) sts, then 14 sts up side of neck, knit 33 (35: 37: 39) sts from holder at back neck, 14 sts down side of left neck, then 9 (10: 11: 12) sts at center left neck. 79 (83: 87: 91) sts

Beg with a purl row, work straight in st st until hood measures 7¾ (8¼: 8¾: 9) in./20 (21: 22: 23) cm, ending with a purl row.

shape top

Bind (cast) off 26 (27: 29: 30) sts (1 st rem on needle), k25 (28: 28: 30), bind (cast) off 26 (27: 29: 30) sts.

Rejoin yarn to rem 26 (29: 29: 31) sts and work 4¾ (5¼: 5¼: 5½) in./12 (13: 13: 14) cm straight from bound-off (cast-off) sts. Bind (cast) off all sts.

assemble hood

Using mattress stitch, sew seams at top of hood.

right front border

Join yarn to bottom of right front edge. With RS facing and using size 4 (3.5 mm) needles, pick up and knit 77 (85: 91: 97) sts along right front edge.

Beg Row 2, work in 1 x 1 rib as for Back as folls:

For boys, work 4 rows in 1 x 1 rib, then bind (cast) off all sts loosely in rib.

For girls, work 1 row in 1 x 1 rib, then work buttonhole row as folls:

K1, p1, k1, k2tog, yo, *rib 8 (9: 10: 11) sts, k2tog, yo, rep from * to last 2 (3: 2: 1) sts, rib to end.

Work 2 more rows in 1 x 1 rib, then bind (cast) off all sts.

left front border

Join yarn to top of left front edge. With RS facing and using size 4 (3.5 mm) needles, pick up and knit 77 (85: 91: 97) sts along left front edge.

Beg Row 2, work in 1 x 1 rib as for Back as folls:

For girls, work 4 rows in 1 x 1 rib, then bind (cast) off all sts loosely in rib.

For boys, work 1 row in 1 x 1 rib, then work buttonhole row as folls:

K1, p1, k1, k2tog, yo, *rib 8 (9: 10: 11) sts, k2tog, yo, rep from * to last 2 (3: 2: 1) sts, rib to end.

Work 2 more rows in 1 x 1 rib, then bind (cast) off all sts.

hood border

Join yarn to hood edge at right front neck. With RS facing and using size 4 (3.5 mm) needles, pick up and knit 41 (44: 46: 48) sts along right edge, pick up and knit 27 (29: 29: 31) sts from top of hood and then 41 (44: 46: 48) sts from left side of hood. Turn and work 4 rows of 1 x 1 rib on these 109 (117: 121: 127) sts. Bind (cast) off all sts loosely in rib.

to finish

Block all pieces. Using mattress stitch, sew up hood border seams to top of front borders. Attach buttons to front border to correspond with buttonholes.

coat

The natural chunkiness of the yarn, combined with a heavyweight stitch, makes it perfect for a coat-style cardigan for those slightly chilly in-between seasons. Knit in a fancy rib, which is an adaptation of a simple 1 x 1 rib, the texture is almost that of a woven fabric. The toggles are an unusual fastening detail and complement the yarn.

materials

5 (5: 6: 7) x 4 oz/100 g balls of Rowan Purelife British Sheep
   Breeds in shade 95 (Black Welsh), 100% wool, 120 yd/110 m
Pair of size 10½ (6.5 mm) knitting needles
Stitch holders
Tapestry (yarn) needle
3 x 1⅛-in./3-cm toggles or 1⅛-in./3-cm diameter buttons
Size H-8 (5 mm) crochet hook

1 large snap fastener
Sewing needle and thread

gauge (tension)

15 sts and 20 rows to 4 in./10 cm over fancy rib on size 10½ (6.5 mm) needles. Always check gauge (tension) carefully, and adjust needle size if necessary (see page 38).

measurements

APPROX. CHEST SIZE	22¾ in./58 cm	24¾ in./63 cm	26¾ in./68 cm	28¾ in./73 cm
ACTUAL CHEST SIZE	26¾ in./68 cm	28¾ in./73 cm	30¾ in./78 cm	33 in./84 cm
ACTUAL LENGTH	14 in./36 cm	16 in./41 cm	18 in./46 cm	19¾ in./50 cm
UNDERARM LENGTH (WITH TURN-UP)	12¼ in./31 cm	13½ in./34 cm	14 in./35 cm	15 in./38 cm

back

Using size 10½ (6.5 mm) needles, cast on 51 (55: 59: 63) sts.

Row 1 (RS): Knit to end.

Row 2: K1, *p1, k1, rep from * to end.

Rep these 2 rows once more, then work Row 1 again.

Row 6: Knit to end.

Row 7: K1, *p1, k1, rep from * to end.

Rows 6 and 7 form fancy rib pattern.

Cont in patt until Back measures 8¼ (9¾: 11½: 12½) in./21 (25: 29: 32) cm or desired length, ending with a WS row.

shape armholes

Bind (cast) off 3 (3: 3: 4) sts at beg of next 2 rows. *45 (49: 53: 55) sts*

Dec one st at each end of next 3 rows, then at each end of every foll alt row until 15 (17: 19: 19) sts rem. Leave sts on holder.

right front

Using size 10½ (6.5 mm) needles, cast on 37 (39: 41: 43) sts.

Row 1: (RS): Knit to end.

Row 2: K1, *p1, k1, rep from * to end.

Work these 2 rows once more, then work Row 1 again.

Row 6: Knit to end.

Row 7: K1, *p1, k1, rep from * to end.

Rows 6 and 7 form fancy rib pattern.

Cont in patt until work measures same as Back to start of armhole shaping, ending with a RS row.

shape armhole

Bind (cast) off 3 (3: 3: 4) sts at beg of next row, then dec 1 st at armhole edge of next 3 rows. *31 (33: 35: 36) sts*

Dec 1 st at armhole edge of every alt row until 21 (22: 23: 23) sts rem, ending with a WS row.

Next row: Bind (cast) off 14 (15: 16: 16) sts, dec 1 st at end of row. *6 sts*

Next row: Dec 1 st at neck edge. *5 sts*

Next row: Dec 1 st at each end of row. *3 sts*

Bind (cast) off rem sts.

left front

Using size 10½ (6.5 mm) needles, cast on 37 (39: 41: 43) sts.

Row 1: Knit to end.

Row 2: K1, *p1, k1, rep from * to end.

Rep these 2 rows once more, then work Row 1 again.

Row 6: Knit to end.

Row 7: K1, *p1, k1, rep from * to end.

Rows 6 and 7 form fancy rib pattern.

Cont in patt until work measures same as Back to start of armhole shaping, ending with a WS row.

shape armhole

Bind (cast) off 3 (3: 3: 4) sts at beg of next row, work 1 row, then dec 1 st at armhole edge of next 3 rows. *31 (33: 35: 36) sts*

Dec 1 st at armhole edge of every alt row until 21 (22: 23: 23) sts rem, ending with a RS row.

Next row: Bind (cast) off 13 (14: 15: 15) sts, patt to end. *8 sts*

Next row: Dec 1 st at each end of row. *6 sts*

Next row: Dec 1 st at neck edge. *5 sts*

Next row: Dec 1 st at each end of row. *3 sts*

Bind (cast) off rem sts.

sleeves (make two alike)

Using size 10½ (6.5 mm) needles, cast on 23 (27: 31: 35) sts.

Row 1 (WS): Knit to end.

Row 2: K1, *p1, k1, rep from * to end.

These two rows form fancy rib pattern.

Cont in patt until work measures 4 (4½: 4¾: 5¼) in./10 (11: 12: 13) cm, ending with a Row 2.

Inc 1 st at each end of next and every foll 6th (6th: 6th: 8th) row until there are 39 (41: 45: 49) sts.

Work straight until sleeve measures 14 (15½: 16¼: 17½) in./36 (39: 41: 44) cm from cast-on, or desired length, ending with a WS row.

(Remember that here the sleeves have been made extra long to allow for turned-up cuffs. You can make the sleeves shorter and omit the cuffs if you wish.)

decrease for raglan sleeve

Bind (cast) off 3 (3: 3: 4) sts at beg of next 2 rows, then dec 1 st at each end of next 3 rows. *27 (29: 33: 35) sts*

Dec 1 st at each end of every alt row until 3 (3: 5: 5) sts rem.

Bind (cast) off all sts.

to finish

Block and press all pieces.

Using mattress stitch, attach sleeves to fronts and back along raglan seams, and sew up side and underarm seams.

Using size 10½ (6.5 mm) needles, attach yarn to right front with RS facing. Pick up and knit 15 (16: 17: 18) sts along front neck, 5 sts up side of neck, 3 (3: 5: 5) sts along sleeve, knit across 15 (17: 19: 19) sts on holder at back neck, then pick up and knit 3 (3: 5: 5) sts from sleeve, 5 sts down side of neck and 15 (16: 17: 18) sts along left front neck. *61 (65: 73: 75) sts*

Turn and work fancy rib as folls:

Row 1: K1, *p1, k1, rep from * to end.

Row 2: Knit to end.

Rep these 2 rows once more, then work Row 1 again.

Bind (cast) off loosely.

Weave in all ends.

girl's coat

For a girl's coat, attach 3 toggles or buttons to left front in a straight line, placing the top one 2⅜ in./6 cm under top of raglan shaping seam and the others about 3 in./8 cm apart. (Be sure to measure to the attachment point, not to the tip of the toggle.)

Using a size H-8 (5 mm) crochet hook, crochet a small chain about 2 in./5 cm long and sew into a loop. Make two more loops the same.

Attach each loop to edge of the front, adjacent to the toggles. Sew one side of a large snap fastener to the underside of the top corner of right front collar and the other half to the corner of the left collar on the right side (this will not be seen, as the right front will overlap it). The fronts will overlap by approx. 3 in./7.5 cm.

boy's coat

For a boy's coat, reverse the positions of the toggles, loops, and snap fastener.

Fold back the sleeves to create cuffs approx 2 (2: 2½: 2½) in./5 (5: 6: 6) cm deep.

accessories

scarf with pockets

This scarf is made using the very simplest of stitches—garter stitch—but after it has been knitted, the ends are folded up and sewn down in a contrasting yarn to create pockets. If your child has very long arms, knit the scarf longer so that he or she can comfortably fit their hands into the pockets.

materials

4 x 2 oz/50 g balls of Debbie Bliss Cashmerino Chunky in shade 23 (purple, yarn A), 55% merino wool, 33% microfiber, 12% cashmere, 71 yd/65 m

1 x 2 oz/50 g ball of Debbie Bliss Cashmerino Chunky in shade 12 (lime green, yarn B) for edging, 55% merino wool, 33% microfiber, 12% cashmere, 71 yd/65 m

Pair of size 10½ (6.5 mm) knitting needles

Tapestry (yarn) needle

gauge (tension)

15 sts and 26 rows to 4 in./10 cm over garter st on size 10½ (6.5 mm) needles. Always check gauge (tension), and adjust needle size if necessary (see page 38).

measurements

Total length of scarf is approx. 55 in./140 cm.

When folded, the scarf is approx. 47 in./120 cm long.

When deciding on the final length, allow for wrapping once around neck; buy one extra ball of yarn for longer scarves.

scarf with pockets

Using size 10½ (6.5mm) needles and yarn B, cast on 24 sts and work 2 rows in garter st (knit every row).

Change to yarn A.

Work in garter stitch until scarf measures 53 in./135 cm or length required.

Change to yarn B.

Knit 2 rows.

Bind (cast) off all stitches.

to finish

Weave in all loose ends.

Fold each short end of scarf back onto the main body of the work to create flaps 6 in./15 cm deep and pin in place.

Using the tapestry (yarn) needle, sew flaps to the main body of the scarf by working decorative blanket stitch down each side in yarn B to create one pocket at each end of the scarf.

hooded scarf

This is a variation on the scarf with pockets, shown on pages 100–101. Here, the scarf is folded in the center and stitched to create a pixy-style hood—perfect for keeping out those icy winter winds! The blanket-stitch edging adds a simple but decorative finishing touch.

materials

4 x 2 oz/50 g balls of Debbie Bliss Cashmerino Chunky in shade 21 (rose, yarn A), 55% merino wool, 33% microfiber, 12% cashmere, 71 yd/65 m

1 x 2 oz/50 g ball of Debbie Bliss Cashmerino Chunky in shade 23 (purple, yarn B) for edging, 55% merino wool, 33% microfiber, 12% cashmere, 71 yd/65 m

Pair of size 10½ (6.5 mm) knitting needles

Tapestry (yarn) needle

gauge (tension)

15 sts and 26 rows to 4 in./10 cm over garter st on size 10½ (6.5 mm) needles. Always check gauge (tension), and adjust needle size if necessary (see page 38).

measurements

Total length of scarf is approx. 55 in./140 cm.

When deciding on the final length, allow for wrapping once around neck; buy one extra ball of yarn for longer scarves.

hooded scarf

Using size 10½ (6.5 mm) needles and yarn A, cast on 24 sts.

Work in garter st (knit every row) until work measures 55 in./140 cm or length required.

Bind (cast) off all stitches.

to finish

Weave in all loose ends.

Fold scarf in half.

On one side, sew together the edges from the fold for about 7 in./18 cm to form the hood.

Using yarn B, work decorative blanket stitch over this join and around all remaining free edges.

ribbed hat

The rib of this hat is a really attractive stitch, yet very simple to do, and it also makes the hat extra warm. The turned-up edge could be made shorter or knitted in a different color; a stripe would also be very effective. Once you've mastered the pattern, therefore, you can knit it many times and make what looks like a different hat each time.

materials

2 x 2 oz/50 g balls of Sublime Extrafine Merino Wool DK in
  0064 (plume), 100% extrafine merino wool, 127 yd/116 m
Pair of size 6 (4 mm) knitting needles
Tapestry (yarn) needle

gauge (tension)

22 sts and 28 rows to 4 in./10 cm over st st on size 6 (4 mm) needles. Always check gauge (tension) carefully, and adjust needle size if necessary (see page 38).

measurements

S (M: L) to fit head up to 19¾ (20¾: 22) in./50 (53: 56) cm.

hat

Using size 6 (4 mm) needles, cast on 114 (118: 126) sts and knit in 2 x 2 rib as folls:
Row 1: K2, *p2, k2, rep from * to end.
Row 2: P2, *k2, p2, rep from * to end.
Rep these 2 rows until work measures 6¼ (7: 7³/₄) in./16 (18: 20) cm from cast-on edge, ending with a Row 2.

decrease for crown

Row 1: [K2, p2, k2tog, p2, k2, p2tog] 9 (9: 10) times, k2, p2, k2tog, [p2, k2] 0 (1: 0) time. 95 (99: 105) sts
Row 2: [P2, k2] 0 (1: 0) time, p1, k2, p2, [k1, p2, k2, p1, k2, p2] 9 (9: 10) times.

Row 3: K2, p2, k1, *p2, k2, p1, k2, p2, k1, rep from * to last 0 (4: 0) sts, [p2, k2] 0 (1: 0) time.
Row 4: [P2, k2] 0 (1: 0) time, p1, k2, p2, *k1, p2, k2, p1, k2, p2, rep from * to end.
Row 5: K2, p1, k2tog, *p2, k1, p2tog, k2, p1, k2tog, rep from * to last 0 (4: 0) sts, [p2, k2] 0 (1: 0) time. 76 (80: 84) sts
Row 6: [P2, k2] 0 (1: 0) time, p1, k1, p2, *k1, p1, k2, p1, k1, p2, rep from * to end.
Row 7: K2, p1, k1, *p2, k1, p1, k2, p1, k1, rep from * to last 0 (4: 0) sts, [p2, k2] 0 (1: 0) time.
Row 8: [P2, k2] 0 (1: 0) time, p1, k1, p2, *k1, p1, k2, p1, k1, p2, rep from * to end.
Row 9: K2tog, p1, k1, *p2tog, k1, p1, k2tog, p1, k1 rep from * to last 0 (4: 0) sts, [p2tog, k2] 0 (1: 0) time. 57 (60: 63) sts
Row 10: P1 (2: 1), *k1, p1, rep from * to end.
Row 11: K3tog, *p1, k1, p1, k3tog, rep from * to last 0 (3: 0) sts, [p1, kk2] 0 (1: 0) time. 37 (40: 41) sts
Row 12: K1 (0: 1), [k2tog] to end. 19 (20: 21) sts

to finish

Break yarn, thread through rem sts using a tapestry (yarn) needle, and pull up tight to form circle.
Sew down seam using mattress stitch, reversing final 3 in./8 cm for fold-back brim.
Weave in ends.
Fold back brim of hat to wear.

ballet bag

The pretty pink stripes on this bag are easy to knit and very effective—and the bag is just perfect for carrying ballet shoes to and from dance classes! Alternatively, you could substitute brighter yarns in your child's school or team colors to make a bag for transporting sports equipment.

materials
1 x 2 oz/50 g ball each of Sirdar Snuggly Bamboo in shades 141 (rosy, yarn A), 142 (cherry lips, yarn B), and 136 (tulip, yarn C), 80% bamboo, 20% wool, 104 yd/95 m
Pair of size 6 (4 mm) knitting needles
Tapestry (yarn) needle
70 in./180 cm cord or ribbon
1 x 1⅛-in./30-mm button
Sewing needle and thread

gauge (tension)
22 sts and 28 rows to 4 in./10 cm over st st on size 6 (4 mm) needles. Always check gauge (tension) carefully, and adjust needle size if necessary (see page 38).

measurements
Bag measures approx. 11 x 13½ in./28 x 34 cm.

ballet bag
Using size 6 (4 mm) needles and yarn A, cast on 64 sts and work in st st throughout, beg with a k row. Work two rows of each color, alternating each in the sequence A, B, C. When work measures 29 in./74 cm from cast-on edge, bind (cast) off all sts.

to finish
Fold the fabric over to the wrong side along the cast-on edge to form a hem ¾ in./2 cm deep. Using the stripes as a guide to keep the hem straight, sew down the hem on the wrong side in mattress stitch. Do not sew down the side edges of the hem, as this is where you thread the cord through. Do the same along the bound-off (cast-off) edge.

Fold the fabric in half so that the hemmed edges meet. Using mattress stitch, sew down the two unhemmed side edges, leaving the hemmed tops free so that you can thread the cord through.

Thread cord through both sides of the hem and knot or sew the ends together to create one loop. The bag can be left threaded through like this, or the cord can be sewn to one bottom corner of bag to create a shoulder strap, as shown in the photos. The cord could also be sewn to both corners of bag to make a backpack. For a pretty, dressed-up bag, use ribbon instead of cord.

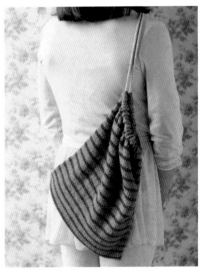

rainbow mittens

Children can often take some persuading to wrap up warmly in the cold weather, but these soft, bright mittens are fun and cozy to wear. If you are worried about one of the mittens getting lost, then crochet or braid (plait) a simple cord to attach the pair together and thread it through the sleeves of Junior's coat.

materials
Debbie Bliss Cashmerino DK 55% merino wool, 33% microfiber, 12% cashmere, 2 oz/50 g, 120 yd/110 m

For pink and red mittens
1 ball each of shades 04 (red, yarn C), 22 (dark pink, yarn D), 27 (light pink, yarn E)

For blue and green mittens
1 ball each of shades 19 (blue, yarn A) and 25 (green, yarn B)

Pair of size 4 (3.5 mm) knitting needles

Pair of size 6 (4 mm) knitting needles

Tapestry (yarn) needle

gauge (tension)
22 sts and 28 rows to 4 in./10 cm over st st on size 6 (4 mm) needles. Always check gauge (tension) carefully, and adjust needle size if necessary (see page 38).

measurements
Actual length of mitten hand is 6 (6¾: 7½) in./15 (17: 19) cm.

color variations

pink and red striped mittens	blue and green striped mittens
Beg in yarn C (red) for rib. When knitting main body of mitten in st st, work throughout in alternate stripes of yarn C, D, and E as folls: 6 rows D 4 rows E 8 rows C Rep these 18 rows throughout pattern.	Beg in yarn A (blue) for rib. When beginning st st, work 4 rows in yarn B (green). Change back to yarn A to complete rest of mitten until work measures 4½ (5¼: 6) in./11 (13: 15) cm from ribbing at wrist. Change back to yarn B and work 4 rows in st st. Return to yarn A and complete shaping for top of mitten.

mittens

Using size 4 (3.5 mm) needles, cast on 37 (39: 41) sts.

Row 1: K1, *p1, k1, rep from * to end of row.

Row 2: P1, *k1, p1, rep from * to end of row.

Rep these two rows of 1 x 1 rib for 1½ (2: 2¾) in./4 (5: 6) cm.
Change to size 6 (4 mm) needles. Beg with a knit row, work 4 (6: 8) rows in st st.

shape thumb

Row 1: K18 (19: 20), m1 by lifting up bar in between sts and knitting it through back of loop, k1, m1, k18 (19: 20). *39 (41: 43) sts*

Row 2 (and every alt row): Purl to end.

Row 3: K18 (19: 20), m1, k3, m1, k18 (19: 20). *41 (43: 45) sts*

Row 5: K18 (19: 20), m1, k5, m1, k18 (19: 20). *43 (45: 47) sts*

Row 7: K18 (19: 20), m1, k7, m1, k18 (19: 20). *45 (47: 49) sts*

Cont to increase in same way, working 2 more sts between the increases, until you have 47 (49: 53) sts, ending with a purl row.

make thumb

Row 1: K29 (30: 33), turn, leaving rem sts unworked.

Row 2: P11 (11: 13), cast on 1 st, turn and cont to work just on these 12 (12: 14) sts.

Work 4 (6: 6) more rows in st st on thumb sts.

Next row: K1, k2tog, k to last 3 sts, sl 1, k1, psso, k1.

Next row: Purl to end.

Rep last 2 rows 1 (1: 2) more times.

Thread yarn through rem sts using tapestry (yarn) needle, pull tight to close opening, secure, and leave yarn for sewing thumb seam.

hand

Rejoin yarn to unworked sts on LH needle and knit rem 18 (19: 20) sts.

Next row: Purl across the 18 (19: 20) sts before thumb, cast on 1 st, and purl across rem 18 (19: 20) sts.

Cont on these 37 (39: 41) sts in st st until work measures 4¾ (5½: 6¼) in./12 (14: 16) cm from beg of ribbing at wrist, ending with a purl row.

shape top of mitten

Row 1: K1, k2tog, k13 (14: 15), sl 1, k1, psso, k1, k2tog, k13 (14: 15), sl 1, k1 psso, k1. *33 (35: 37) sts*

Row 2 (and every alt row): Purl to end.

Row 3: K1, k2tog, k11 (12: 13), sl 1, k1, psso, k1, k2tog, k11 (12: 13), sl 1, k1 psso, k1. *29 (31: 33) sts*

Row 5: K1, k2tog, k9 (10: 11), sl 1, k1, psso, k1, k2tog, k9 (10: 11), sl 1, k1, psso, k1. *25 (27: 29) sts*

Row 7: K1, k2tog, k7 (8: 9), sl 1, k1, psso, k1, k2tog, k7 (8: 9), sl 1, k1 psso, k1. *21 (23: 25) sts*

Row 8: Purl to end.

to finish

Break yarn and thread through rem sts using a tapestry (yarn) needle, pull up tight to form circle, and secure.
Sew down side seam using mattress stitch.
Sew up thumb seam.

cord (optional)

To join the mittens together with a cord, using yarn used for the rib, crochet, twist, or braid (plait) a length slightly longer than your child's arm span, then sew one end of the cord to rib at side seam of each mitten.

hat with ear flaps

The flaps on this hat keep the head and ears warm and cozy and also look extremely cute. The traditional-style braided (plaited) tassels can be tied to stop the hat from blowing off or left loose as a style statement.

materials
1 x 2 oz/ 50 g ball of Sublime Organic Merino DK in shade 19 (asparagus, yarn A), 100% organic merino wool, 113 yd/105m
1 x 2 oz/ 50 g ball of Sublime Organic Merino DK in shade 17 (saltwater, yarn B), 100% organic merino wool, 113 yd/105 m
Pair of size 8 (5 mm) knitting needles
Stitch holders
Tapestry (yarn) needle

gauge (tension)
18 sts and 26 rows to 4 in./10 cm over st st on size 8 (5 mm) needles. Always check gauge (tension) carefully, and adjust needle size if necessary (see page 38).

measurements
S (M: L) to fit head up to 19¼ (20½: 21½) in./49 (52: 55) cm.

ear flaps (make two alike)
Using size 8 (5 mm) needles and yarn A, cast on 5 sts.
Row 1: Knit to end
Row 2: Inc 1, k to last st, inc 1. *7 sts*
Rep these 2 rows until there are 21 (23: 25) sts.
Work straight in garter st until flap measures 3 (3½: 4) in./8 (9: 10) cm from cast-on edge.
Leave 21 (23: 25) sts for flap on holder.

hat
Using size 8 (5 mm) needles and yarn A, cast on 12 sts, knit across 21 (23: 25) sts of one ear flap, cast on 24 (26: 28) sts, knit across 21 (23: 25) sts of rem ear flap, cast on 12 sts.

90 (96: 102) sts
Work 1½ in./4 cm in garter st on these 90 (96: 102) sts.
Change to yarn B. Cont in st st until work measures 4 (4¾: 5½) in./10 (12: 14) cm from cast-on for hat, ending with a purl row.

decrease for crown
Row 1: *K4, k2tog, rep from * to end of row. *75 (80: 85) sts*
Beg with a purl row, work 3 rows in st st.
Row 5: *K3, k2tog, rep from * to end of row. *60 (64: 68) sts*
Beg with a purl row, work 3 rows in st st.
Row 9: *K2, k2tog, rep from * to end of row. *45 (48: 51) sts*
Row 10: Purl to end.
Row 11: *K1, k2tog, rep from * to end of row. *30 (32: 34) sts*
Row 12: Purl to end.
Row 13: K2tog across row. *15 (16: 17) sts*
Row 14: Purl to end.

to finish
Break yarn and thread through rem sts using a tapestry (yarn) needle, pull up tight to form circle, and secure. Sew down back seam using mattress stitch. Weave in ends.

tassels
Using yarn A, cut nine strands of yarn 18 in./45 cm long and knot together at one end. Separate into three sections of three strands of yarn each and braid (plait). Knot at bottom and trim into shape.
Repeat to make a second tassel.
Attach one tassel to bottom of each ear flap as decoration or to use as a fastening.

teddy to treasure

Every child needs a well-loved, worn teddy, and this pattern aims to capture the best aspects of an heirloom bear. With his crooked smile, button eyes, and soft tummy, he simply cries out to be cuddled.

materials

2 x 2 oz/50 g balls of Sublime Cashmere Merino Silk DK in shade 11 (clove, yarn A), 75% extrafine merino wool, 20% silk, 5% cashmere, 127 yd/116 m

1 x 2 oz/50 g ball of Sublime Cashmere Merino Silk DK in shade 03 (vanilla, yarn B), 75% extrafine merino wool, 20% silk, 5% cashmere, 127 yd/116 m

Pair of size 6 (4 mm) needles

Toy stuffing

Tapestry (yarn) needle

Small amounts of brown yarn C for embroidery

2 buttons of whichever size you desire for eyes

Sewing needle and thread

gauge (tension)

Gauge (tension) is not critical here, but as a guide, 22 sts and 28 rows to 4 in./10 cm over st st on size 6 (4 mm) needles.

measurements

The bear measures approx. 17¾ in./45 cm from head to toe.

teddy
circles for end of arms/legs and for ears

Make two alike in yarn A for ears and make four alike in yarn B for arms/legs.

Using size 6 (4 mm) needles, cast on 5 sts.

Row 1: Inc 1, k to last st, inc 1. *7 sts*

Row 2 (and every alt row): Purl to end.

Row 3: Inc 1, k to last st, inc 1. *9 sts*

Row 5: Inc 1, k to last st, inc 1. *11 sts*

Row 7: Knit to end.

Row 9: K2tog, k to last 2 sts, k2tog. *9 sts*

Row 11: K2tog, k to last 2 sts, k2tog. *7 sts*

Row 13: K2tog, k to last 2 sts, k2tog. *5 sts*

Bind (cast) off all sts.

arms and left leg (make three alike)

Using size 6 (4 mm) needles and yarn A, cast on 28 sts.

Work 8 rows in st st, beg with a k row.

On next and every foll 4th row, dec 1 st at each end until 12 sts rem.

Beg with a purl row, work 2 rows in st st.

Break yarn, thread through rem sts using a tapestry (yarn) needle, and pull up to close opening. Secure and sew down arm seam using mattress stitch. Stuff tube with toy stuffing, Sew a circle in yarn B onto end, with purl side facing outward.

right leg (make one)

Using size 6 (4 mm) needles and yarn A, cast on 28 sts.

Knit 8 rows in st st, beg with a k row.

On next and every foll 6th row, dec 1 st at each end until 14 sts rem.

Beg with a purl row, work 2 rows in st st.

Break yarn, thread through rem sts using a tapestry (yarn) needle, and pull up to close opening. Secure and sew down arm seam using mattress stitch. Stuff tube with toy stuffing. Sew a circle in yarn B onto end, with purl side facing outward.

head

Using size 6 (4 mm) needles and yarn A, cast on 20 sts.

Row 1: [K1, inc in next st] across row. *30 sts*

Row 2 (and every alt row): Purl to end.

Row 3: [K2, inc in next st] across row. *40 sts*

Row 5: [K3, inc in next st] across row. *50 sts*

Beg and ending with a purl row, work in st st on these 50 sts for 3 in./8 cm.

crown

Row 1: [K4, inc in next st] across row. *60 sts*

Row 2 (and every alt row): Purl to end.

Row 3: [K5, inc in next st] across row. *70 sts*

Beg with a purl row, work 5 rows in st st.

Row 9: [K5, k2tog] across row. *60 sts*

Row 11: [K4, k2tog] across row. *50 sts*

Row 13: [K3, k2tog] across row. *40 sts*

Row 15: [K2, k2tog] across row. *30 sts*

Row 17: [K1, k2tog] across row. *20 sts*

Row 19: K2tog across row. *10 sts*

Break yarn.

Thread yarn through rem sts using a tapestry (yarn) needle, and pull up to close opening.

Secure and then sew down head seam using mattress stitch.

Stuff head evenly with toy stuffing.

Thread yarn around cast-on edge and pull up to close hole.

Secure with a few stitches, then weave in ends.

body

Using size 6 (4 mm) needles and yarn A, cast on 10 sts.

Row 1: Inc in every st across row. *20 sts*

Row 2 (and every alt row): Purl to end.

Row 3: [K1, inc in next st] across row. *30 sts*

Row 5: [K2, inc in next st] across row. *40 sts*

Row 7: [K3, inc in next st] across row. *50 sts*

Row 9: [K4, inc in next st] across row. *60 sts*

Starting and ending with a purl row, work in st st on these 60 sts for 4 in./10 cm.

dec for neck

Row 1: [K4, k2tog] across row. *50 sts*

Row 2 (and every foll alt row): Purl to end.

Row 3: [K3, k2tog] across row. *40 sts*

Row 5: [K2, k2tog] across row. *30 sts*

Row 7: [K1, k2tog] across row. *20 sts*

Row 9: K2tog across row. *10 sts*

Break yarn, thread through rem sts using a tapestry (yarn) needle, and pull up to close opening. Secure and then sew down body seam using mattress stitch. Stuff body evenly with toy stuffing. Thread yarn around cast-on edge and pull up to close hole. Secure with a few stitches, then weave in ends.

to finish

Sew head, arms, and legs securely onto body. Fold ear circles in half and sew along edges to create two closed semicircles. Sew semicircles into top of head. Sew buttons onto head for eyes. Embroider a mouth and nose by couching or backstitching, using brown yarn C.

lace beret

This simple beret uses a very basic laceholes pattern to add texture to a classic shape.

materials

1 x 2 oz/50 g ball each of RYC Cashsoft Aran in shades 24 (fuchsia, yarn A) and 002 (lilac, yarn B), 57% extrafine merino, 33% microfiber, 10% cashmere, 95 yd/87 m
Pair each of size 6 (4 mm) and size 8 (5 mm) knitting needles
Tapestry (yarn) needle

gauge (tension)

17 sts and 25 rows to 4 in./10 cm over st st on size 8 (5 mm) needles. Always check gauge (tension) carefully, and adjust needle size if necessary (see page 38).

measurements

S (M: L) to fit head up to 19½ (20¾: 22) in./50 (53: 56) cm.

beret

Using size 6 (4 mm) needles and yarn A, cast on 82 (86: 92) sts and work 6 rows of 1 x 1 rib as folls:
Row 1: *K1, p1, rep from * to end of row.
Rep this row 5 more times, inc into last st of last row on medium size only and inc 1 st at each end of row on small and large sizes only. *84 (87: 94) sts*
Next row: K2 (2: 7), m1 by picking up the bar between sts and knitting it, *k2, m1, rep from * to last 2 (1: 7) sts, k2 (1: 7). *125 (130: 135) sts*
Change to size 8 (5 mm) needles.
Next row: Purl to end.
Next row: K1, m1, *k5, m1, rep to last 4 sts, k4. *150 (156: 162) sts*
Change to yarn B and purl one row.

lace hole section

Row 1: K0 (1: 0), *k2, k2tog, yo, rep from * to last 2 (3: 2) sts, k2 (3: 2).
Rows 2–4: Work 3 rows in st st beg with a purl row.
Row 5: K0 (1: 1), *k2tog, yo, k2, rep from * ending last rep k2 (1: 2).
Rows 6–8: Work 3 rows in st st, beg with a purl row.
Rep Rows 1–5 once more.
Next row: Purl to end.

decrease for crown

Row 1: *K4, k2tog, rep from * to end of row. *125 (130: 135) sts*
Work 5 rows in st st, beg with a purl row.
Row 7: *K3, k2tog, rep from * to end of row. *100 (104: 108) sts*
Work 3 rows in st st, beg with a purl row.
Change to yarn A.
Work 2 rows in st st beg with a knit row.
Row 13: *K2, k2tog, rep from * to end of row. *75 (78: 81) sts*
Work 5 rows in st st beg with a purl row.
Row 19: *K1, k2tog, rep from * to end of row. *50 (52: 54) sts*
Row 20 (small and medium sizes): P2 (3) tog, p to last 2 (3) sts, p2 (3) tog. *48 sts*
Row 20 (large size): Purl to end. *54 sts*
Row 21: *K4, k2tog, rep from * to end of row. *40 (40: 45) sts*
Row 22 (and every alt row): Purl to end.
Row 23: *K3, k2tog, rep from * to end of row. *32 (32: 36) sts*
Row 25: *K2, k2tog, rep from * to end of row. *24 (24: 27) sts*
Row 27: *K1, k2tog, rep from * to end of row. *16 (16: 18) sts*
Row 29: [K2tog] across row. *8 (8: 9) sts*

to finish

Break yarn, thread through rem sts using a tapestry (yarn) needle, pull up tight, and secure to join in round. Sew down seam using mattress stitch and weave in ends.

simple socks

Socks are a fantastic small, quick, and portable project. This makes them seriously addictive, so beware: once you have mastered the technique, you will be making more pairs of socks than you can give away! This pattern is the simplest sock you can make and can be adapted to create striped socks or longer or shorter socks as you wish.

materials

Regia 4-ply Wool Sock Yarn, 75% superwash new wool, 25% polyamide, 2 oz/50 g, 229 yd/210 m or Regia 4-ply Silk Sock yarn, 55% new wool, 25% polyamide, 20% silk, 2 oz/50 g, 218 yd/200 m

for blue socks
1 ball of Regia 4-ply Wool in shade 1988 (dark blue, yarn A)
1 ball of Regia 4-ply Silk in shade 54 (light blue, yarn B)

for yellow socks
1 ball of Regia 4-ply Wool in shade 1092 (green, yarn A)
1 ball of Regia 4-ply Wool in shade 2060, (yellow, yarn B)
Set of size 1 (2.5 mm) double-pointed needles
Set of size 2 (3 mm) double-pointed needles

gauge (tension)

33 sts and 40 rows over 4 in./10 cm over st st on size 2 (3 mm) needles. Always check gauge (tension) carefully, and adjust needle size if necessary (see page 38).

measurements

S (M: L)
Actual foot length: 6 (6½: 7½) in./15 (16.5: 19) cm

socks

Using size 1 (2.5 mm) double-pointed needles, cast on 42 (48: 54) sts in yarn A and join for working in the round.
Work 6 rounds in 1 x 1 rib as folls:
Rnd 1: *K1, p1, rep from * to end of round.
Rep this round 5 more times.
Change to yarn B and size 2 (3 mm) needles.
Work 2½ (3¼: 4) in./6 (8: 10) cm in st st (knit every round, see page 32).

divide for heel

Change to yarn A and knit across 21 (23: 27) sts. Leave rem 21 (25: 27) sts unknitted on one dpn for instep.

Work 21 (23: 27) sts for heel straight on 2 needles as folls:

Row 1: Sl 1p, p to end.

Row 2: Sl 1k, k to end.

Work these 2 rows 7 (9: 11) more times. *16 (20: 24) rows*

Next row: Rep Row 1. *17 (21: 24) rows*

turn heel

Row 1: K13 (15: 17), sl 1, k1, psso, k1, turn, leaving rem sts unworked.

Row 2: Sl 1, p6 (8: 8), p2tog, p1, turn.

Row 3: Sl 1, k7 (9: 9), sl 1, k1, psso, k1, turn.

Row 4: Sl 1, p8 (10: 10), p2tog, p1, turn.

Row 5: Sl 1, k9 (11: 11), sl 1, k1, psso, k1, turn.

Row 6: Sl 1, p10 (12: 12), p2tog, p1, turn.

Row 7: Sl 1, k11 (13: 13), sl 1, k1, psso, k0 (0: 1), turn.

Row 8: Sl 0 (0: 1), p12 (14: 14), p2tog, p0 (0: 1), turn.

Heel stitches of small and medium sizes are now all worked.

large size only:

Row 9: Sl 1, k15, sl 1, k1, psso, turn.

Row 10: P16, p2tog.

Heel stitches of large size are now all worked.

all sizes:

13 (15: 17) sts rem on needle.

K7 (8: 9) sts and leave on one dpn; this completes the heel. Change to yarn B and knit rem 6 (7: 8) sts in yarn B with extra dpn to work in the round. With same needle, pick up and knit 9 (11: 13) sts along side of heel. (The slipped stitches at the beg of rows will help you to see where to pick up the stitches.) With second dpn, knit across instep.

With 3rd dpn, pick up and knit 9 (11: 13) sts along other side of heel, k 7 (8: 9) sts of heel. (Remember that the last st of 3rd needle is the last st of the round.) *52 (62: 70) sts*

Knit 1 round straight as outlined.

shape instep

Round 1: Knit to last 3 sts of first dpn, k2tog, k1; knit across all sts of instep on 2nd dpn; on 3rd dpn k1, sl 1, k1, psso, k to end of needle. *50 (60: 68) sts*

Round 2: Knit to end.

Rep these 2 rounds until 42 (50: 54) sts rem.

Cont on these sts working straight in st st in the round until work measures 3 (3½: 4½) in./8 (9: 11) cm from heel (measure from the darker color of heel).

Fasten off yarn B.

shape toe

Change to yarn A.

Round 1: Knit to end.

Round 2: K to last 3 sts of first dpn, k2tog, k1; on 2nd dpn k1, sl 1, k1, psso, k to last 3 sts on needle, k2tog, k1; on 3rd needle k1, sl 1, k1, psso, k to end of rnd.

Rep these 2 rounds until 22 (26: 26) sts rem.

to finish

The sock is now complete apart from binding (casting) off.

To prevent bulky toe seams, it is best to close the seam while binding (casting) off. To do this, work from the wrong side of the sock as folls:

With wrong side showing, distribute the sts evenly on two dpns, so that the back and front of toe are on separate needles; hold both needles together in left hand. With a 3rd dpn, knit through both first sts on the needles, as if you are knitting 2 sts together normally. Do the same with next 2 sts so there are 2 sts on right-hand needle and bind (cast) off as usual, leaving one st on right-hand needle. Continue in this way until all sts are bound (cast) off. Fasten off yarn.

animal slippers

These instructions are for a sweet little rabbit, but you could adapt the ear shape to make dogs, cats, or anything you desire—perhaps to match a beloved pet!

materials

1 x 2 oz/50 g ball of Sirdar Eco Wool DK in shade 202 (clay), 203 (earth), or 204 (flint), 100% wool, 109 yd/100 m (yarn A)
Small amounts of any contrasting yarn for ears and embellishments (yarn B)
Pair each of size 6 (4 mm) and size 7 (4.5 mm) knitting needles
4 buttons under ⅜ in./10 mm in diameter for eyes
Tapestry (yarn) needle, sewing needle and sewing thread

gauge (tension)

22 sts and 38 rows to 4 in./10 cm over garter st on size 6 (4 mm) needles. Always check gauge (tension) carefully, and adjust needle size if necessary (see page 38).

measurements

Actual length of slippers is approx. 4 (5½: 6¾) in./10 (14: 17) cm.

slippers

Using size 6 (4 mm) needles and yarn A, cast on 28 (36: 44) sts.
Work in garter st until work measures 2¾ (3½: 4½) in./7 (9: 11) cm.

decrease for toe

Row 1: K2tog, k to last 2 sts, k2tog. *26 (34: 42) sts*
Row 2 (and every alt row): Knit to end.
Rep these two rows until 2 sts rem. Bind (cast) off rem sts.

edging

Using size 6 (4 mm) needles and yarn A, pick up and knit 18 (22: 26) sts along one straight side, then work 4 rows in 2 x 2 rib on these sts. Bind (cast) off in rib.
Rep along other straight side.

to finish

Fold down the point at bound-off (cast-off) edge of work to the center of the row where toe decreasing begs. Fold in both sides, so that the garter st row ends meet in the middle; the ribbed edges will stand upright. Sew along the two diagonal seams where the point folds in on itself, then up the ribbing seam, but leave the long straight side seams free. At the heel end of the slipper, sew down from top of the rib to about ½ in./1.5 cm from the bottom. Push the unstitched part of the heel up to meet the central seam, with the same amount of fabric extending on each side, to create an upside-down T shape. Sew along the resulting seams.

ears

Work two alike in yarn A and two alike in yarn B.
Using size 7 (4.5 mm) needles, cast on 3 sts.
Row 1: Inc 1, k to last st, inc 1. *5 sts*
Row 2 (and every alt row): Purl to end.
Row 3: Inc 1, k to last st, inc 1. *7 sts*
Row 5: Knit to end.
Row 7: Knit to end.
Row 9: K2tog, k to last 2 sts, k2tog. *5 sts*
Row 11: K2tog, k to last 2 sts, k2tog. *3 sts*
Row 13: K3tog.
Fasten off rem st.

to finish

Place one ear in yarn A and and one in yarn B together, with purl sides facing. Sew all around edges to join and then attach to front of slipper. Sew on buttons for eyes and embroider a mouth and nose using yarn B.

caring for woollens

Handmade items need special care, and knitted ones are no different, even if the yarns used in this book are machine washable. The fact that the yarns are a special blend of natural and synthetic fibers means that you don't have to treat them as delicately as pure wools, as they are unlikely to felt and shrink to nothing and will hold their shape better; however, they are still prone to stretching and pulling, just like any other knitted garment. You may wish to hand wash more delicate items, regardless of the washing instructions on the yarn label. However, all items should, where possible, be washed on a delicate or cool wash. In addition, you should avoid giving knitted items a final spin in the washing machine, as they are prone to becoming misshapen, especially when wet.

Instead of spinning the garment, remove it from the machine and place it on a dry towel. Roll up the towel with the garment inside, and apply pressure to squeeze out excess water without pulling it out of shape. You may need to do this several times, but when the garment is less sodden, you can then lay it out flat to dry on a dry towel. Knitted garments should not be hung up to dry; gravity does its worst and the article of clothing can stretch out of shape. This is why you should not pin it to a clothes line, especially as clothespins will also leave stretch marks in knitting. When the item is dry, you can use a cool steam iron to smooth it out—but do not apply pressure, as this will flatten the yarn and stitches. Finally, fold and place the garment in a drawer or closet, away from the moths!

suppliers

Contact the manufacturer or distributor listed below for details of stockists in your area.

MANUFACTURERS AND DISTRIBUTORS— UNITED KINGDOM

DEBBIE BLISS YARNS

Designer Yarns
Unit 8–10
Newbridge Industrial Estate
Pitt Street
Keighley
West Yorkshire BD21 4PQ
Tel: 01535 664222
www.designeryarns.uk.com

MISSION FALLS YARNS

Hantex Ltd
Unit 1 Whitehouse
Business Units
Eaudyke
Friskney
Lincolnshire PE22 8NL
Tel: 01754 820800
www.hantex.co.uk

ROWAN YARNS

Rowan
Green Lane Mill
Holmfirth
West Yorkshire HD9 2DX
Tel: 01484 681881
www.knitrowan.com

SIRDAR YARNS

Sirdar Spinning Ltd
Flanshaw Lane
Wakefield
West Yorkshire WF2 9ND
Tel: 01924 371501
www.sirdar.co.uk

SUBLIME YARNS

Tel: 01924 369666
www.sublimeyarns.com

GENERAL STOCKISTS— UNITED KINGDOM

LOOP

41 Cross St
London N1 2BB
Tel: 020 7288 1160
www.loop.gb.com

JOHN LEWIS

Tel: 08456 049 049
www.johnlewis.com

MANUFACTURERS AND DISTRIBUTORS— UNITED STATES

DEBBIE BLISS YARNS

Knitting Fever Inc.
PO Box 336
315 Bayview Avenue
Amityville
NY 11701
Tel: 516 546 3600
www.knittingfever.com

MISSION FALLS YARNS

CNS Yarns
c/o Milgram
156 Lawrence Paquette
Champlain
NY 12919
www.cnsyarns.com

ROWAN YARNS

Westminster Fibers
165 Ledge Street
Nashua
NH 03060
Tel: 603 886 5041
www.westminsterfibers.com

SIRDAR YARNS

Knitting Fever Inc.
PO Box 336
315 Bayview Avenue
Amityville
NY 11701
Tel: 516 546 3600
www.knittingfever.com
export@sirdar.co.uk

MANUFACTURERS AND DISTRIBUTORS— CANADA

DEBBIE BLISS YARNS

Diamond Yarn Ltd
155 Martin Ross Avenue
Unit 3
Toronto
Ontario M3J 2L9
Tel: 416 736 6111
web: www.diamondyarn.com

MISSION FALLS YARNS

Head Office
5333 Casgrain #1204
Montreal
Quebec H2T 1X3
Toll free: 877 244 1204
Other inquiries: 514 276 1204
www.missionfalls.com

ROWAN YARNS

Diamond Yarn Ltd
155 Martin Ross Avenue
Unit 3
Toronto
Ontario M3J 9L0
Tel: 416 736 6111
www.diamondyarn.com

SIRDAR YARNS

Diamond Yarn Ltd
155 Martin Ross Avenue
Unit 3
Toronto
Ontario M3J 2L9
Tel: 416 736 6111
www.diamondyarn.com
export@sirdar.co.uk